A Folded History

A Folded History:
Poems and Mythologies

Edited by Philip Walsh and Rachel Hadas

Illustrations by Emma Hunter

RAGGED SKY PRESS
PRINCETON, NEW JERSEY

The poems and postludes published in this book first appeared in a special issue of *The Classical Outlook* 99.3 (2024). The editors would like to thank Sherwin Little, Executive Director of the American Classical League, and Jennie Luongo, President of the American Classical League, for their support of this project. We would also like to thank the Department of Classics at Princeton University, which organized an event celebrating the publication of the special issue in January 2025.

Finally, the editors would like to dedicate this book to their students: past, present, and future.

Copyright ©2025 by Philip Walsh and Rachel Hadas
All rights reserved
Published by Ragged Sky Press
www.raggedsky.com
Library of Congress Control Number: 2025939572
ISBN: 978-1-933974-61-3
Cover design: Jean Foos
Interior and cover art: Emma Hunter

Printed in the United States of America
First Edition

Contents

Introduction. "The Folded History of Old Rivers" / Rachel Hadas | 1

γῆρας προσδέχου / Jordi Alonso | 3

Diana's Arrow / Catherine Anderson | 4

A Different Growth / Josephine Balmer | 6

A Pig's Eye / Al Basile | 7

The Roman Portraits / Meredith Bergmann | 9

Psyche Revisits the Closet of Venus / Meredith Bergmann | 10

A Bottle (According to Aristotle) / Elijah Perseus Blumov | 11

When Icarus Fell / David Capps | 13

Aristotle at Pyrrha / Christopher Childers | 14

This Is No Longer Troy / Terese Coe | 17

The Death of Aegeus / Armand D'Angour | 19

Achilles' Heel / David Franklin | 22

Liber Tertius Decimus / Julia Griffin | 22

Briseis Weeps for Patroclus / Julia Griffin | 23

A Calm Cassandra / Katie Hartsock | 25

A Plague of Our Own Making / Andrew Hudgins | 26

The Shade of Heracles / Dax Johnson | 28

The Goddess Drusilla / Larry Johnson | 29

The Handbook of Epictetus / George Kalogeris | 30

Scylla and Charybdis / George Kalogeris | 31

After the Fall / David M. Katz | 32

Philoctetes / Karl Kirchwey | 33

"When Philoctetes in the Lemnian Isle"/ Karl Kirchwey | 34

Caesar and the Rose / Rachel A. Lott | 37

On the Gift of the Cyclops / Charles Martin | 38

On the Afterlife / Charles Martin | 39

Of Prey and Predators / Charles Martin | 40

The Chorus / Zachary McGar | 42

Achilles and Odysseus / Susan McLean | 43

Meditatio / Geoffrey Movius | 45

Herakles / Julia Nemirovskaya (Boris Dralyuk, trans.) | 46

Your Eyes, / Suzanne Noguere | 47

Tiresias in Hell / Eugene O'Connor | 48

On First Reading the Loeb Catullus, Carmen 64 / Saffron Orffas | 49

Love Poem as Abandoned Greek Soldier / James Owens | 52

Corinna Comes, Once Again / Basil Perkins | 53

At the Library of the Baths of Trajan / Trish Reeves | 54

The Roses of Heliogabalus / Dan Rosenberg | 56

Athena's Owl / Robert B. Shaw | 58

Rendering *Aeneid* 3.415 / R. Allen Shoaf | 61

Miasma / Gerald Smith | 63

Ganymede / William E. Smith III | 65

Prelude to an Aubade / C. Luke Soucy | 67

Sappho at the Beach / David Southward | 68

Hippiad: A Verse Lecture / A. E. Stallings | 70

After Her Party / Timothy Steele | 73

At the Jetty / Linda Stern | 74

Jason / Henry Stimpson | 75

The Ex-Wife Becomes Galatea / Eileen R. Tabios | 77

Face in the Mantle / N. S. Thompson | 78

The Combatants / Daniel Tobin | 80

Alexandria Redux / Wyatt Townley | 82

He Was on Leave / Joyce Wilson | 83

Odyssey 5 / Jessica Wood | 84

Dwelling in Possibility: A Dialogue between Editor and
    Artist, Student and Teacher | 87

"The Folded History of Old Rivers":
On Poetry and Postludes

Rachel Hadas
Poetry Editor, *The Classical Outlook*
rhadas@rutgers.edu

Among the nearly fifty writers whose work is gathered here are a sculptor, a philosopher, many teachers and professors, a graduate student or two, and two undergraduates. They hail from many parts of the United States, from Canada, from the UK, and from South Africa. Many of them have translated from Greek or Latin or both; several of them tutor new arrivals in the United States in English. All of them, obviously, are poets. And all are lovers of the classics, enthusiasts whose work radiates the discoveries and surprises, the joys and connections, that classical literature, mythology, and art have continued to bestow for centuries – gifts that keep on giving now, in the twenty-first century, and that continue to be a source of personal enrichment and poetic inspiration.

Assembling the poems for this issue has reminded me that the pleasures of engaging with classical literature are not only robustly durable, they're also contagious. For these poems offer connections to authors, texts, or works of art that readers might not have thought of, at least not in the particular context each poem provides. An incomplete list of the authors these poems refer to includes Homer, Aristotle, Epictetus, Ovid, Propertius, Horace, and Vergil. Turn to the postludes – the prose accompaniment the poets have been asked to provide – and the list expands. As the poets wrote their poems, they were thinking of works by Angelos Sikelianos, Cesare Pavese, W. H. Auden, Derek Mahon, William Carlos Williams, Agha Shahid Ali, A. E. Stallings, Barbara Ehrenreich, Marguerite Yourcenar, and Madeline Miller. They were pondering the many horses and mules in the *Iliad*; Roman portrait busts; the library at Alexandria; Scylla and Charybdis; Ganymede; Icarus; Tiresias; and Galatea. Their inspirations included Athena's owl, the river Meander, Psyche, Cinderella, Rumpelstiltskin. As well as such archetypal images and figures, the poets paid close attention to an Egyptian inscription, a local swimming pool, a glimpsed pedestrian too frightened to cross the street, a neighbor remembered from childhood, a beloved house. Sometimes the poets revised familiar versions of myth. The possibilities, I came to see, were endless. As gathered poems often do, serendipitously or otherwise, these poems seem to speak to one another. I hope that they will not only give pleasure to the readers of *The Classical Outlook* but will also inspire more poems.

Another hope this project has nurtured is my newfound wish that more journals and periodicals that publish poetry asked the poets to give some account of what they were doing. Such prose commentary is often enlightening; it's also highly individual and frequently unexpected. Poets seem to relish revisiting the occasion that first inspired a poem – a poem that may have undergone multiple alterations and iterations before it ever left their desk. Such revisiting of a poem's genesis may take the poet back to a course they took or a class they taught; local history they learned; an island they visited; a movie they saw; a dream; a house they built; a difficult relationship that turns out, in the light of the right classical text, to have been a source of inspiration. One never knows quite what led to the birth of a poem; I suspect these poets often didn't know themselves, until someone asked them. The postludes provide a dazzlingly varied showcase of some of the myriad ways poems come into being.

The notion of a postlude reminds me of David Lehman's excellent 1986 anthology, *Ecstatic Occasions, Expedient Forms*. In editing this anthology, Lehman asked his contributors to supply brief accounts of the formal considerations that had gone into the crafting of their poems. More recent poetry anthologies also have recourse to the notion of a postlude. Lehman, Series Editor of the excellent *Best American Poetry* series, has continued to ask the contributing poets for brief prose accompaniments. And Erin Belieu and Carl Phillips's 2023 anthology, *Personal Best: Makers on Their Poems That Matter Most*, carries on this practice.

In editing *Ecstatic Occasions, Expedient Forms*, David Lehman took his book's title from Marianne Moore's dictum about poetry: "Ecstasy affords the occasion, and expediency determines the form." The poems in this special issue represent both plenty of ecstasy and a wealth of formal procedures; the poets have shaped their communings with the classical legacy into sonnets, villanelles, a sestina, and many flavors of free verse. They have felt free to approach their subject matter in widely differing ways. Some have sent me back to a classical text

– the *Iliad*, say, or Ovid's *Amores*, or Catullus 64, among others. There's always more to learn, both about individual poets and about the classical works that have nourished their imaginations. Illumination, enlightenment, and connection are constant.

My own poetic engagement with classical texts dates back to a poem I wrote in high school, where I first studied Latin, about Dido and Aeneas emerging from the cave a storm has driven them to seek shelter in – and we know what followed. A few years later, images of the restless Trojans penned inside their walls fed into an elegy for my father. Later still, living on the island of Samos and learning Modern Greek brought me closer to stories and landscapes I'd only ever read about and imagined. More recently, following the 2016 election, I turned back to the *Aeneid*, especially the second half of the epic, for inspiration for a series of poems imbued with ominous images of war and civil strife. My current project, a prosimetrum or mix of poetry and prose, juxtaposes poems variously inspired by mythology, poems which I've written over the past thirty years, with brief postludes all dating from 2023. Read together, these prose interludes turned out to constitute a kind of memoir, bringing back classrooms and conversations, travels and dreams I thought I'd forgotten, and putting these fleeting memories into a thematic framework.

Mona Van Duyn has written that myth affords "simultaneous discovery and reminiscence." The myth-inspired poems in this issue, and the prose reflections that accompany them, offer a wealth of layers of discovery enriched by memory. That this palimpsest provides a rich environment for imagination and metaphor is a recurrent theme in the varied postludes that accompany the poems gathered here. It's a theme expressed with particular eloquence in the postlude to "Miasma," whose author Gerald Smith, Professor Emeritus of Religion and Environmental Studies at the University of the South, submitted the passage I'll close by quoting, in the hope that the readers of *The Classical Outlook* will take the time to savor it, as well as all the poems and postludes that follow:

> The folded history of old rivers . . . seemed an apt image of my academic life as I closed my teaching career which I described this way in my last lecture: "Sewanee is a river flowing along and leaving in its curves the meanders of history. Meanders become oxbow lakes and are cut off from the main channel. In time the oxbows become swamps or bogs and eventually fill in and disappear as active parts of the main river. The river bends again and flows elsewhere even while the meanders and oxbows remain as the braided history of sedimentation – or in the case of this analogy – remain as the textured history of old classes and old professors which have now been overlaid and supplanted by the new life of the flowing river of learning . . . The river is moving on, folding what I have done into the life, memory, and then in time, into the forgetfulness of this place." Meanders and the associated miasmas of river bottoms have supplied a rich metaphorical source for my teachings about both history and nature.

I'll add yet another layer not specified, though perhaps implied, by Smith in this passage: His poem "Miasma" is a kind of riff or midrash on a couplet from an elegy by Propertius. Such are the sedimentary layers of poetry, where all kinds of knowledge and experience, textual and personal, can meet in an unexpected and often generative encounter.

It has been a great pleasure to work on this issue with Phil Walsh, the Editor of *The Classical Outlook*. Phil's energy, attentiveness, and good sense have made collaborating with him not only easy but delightful. The excellent idea of postludes to each poem was Phil's, and I'm grateful to him for that, as for much else. Phil and I are both indebted to our colleague, Diane Arnson Svarlien, for her early support of this special issue and for her superb editorial judgment. I'm proud of our distinguished and eclectic lineup of poets – both poets whose names and work may be familiar to readers of *The Classical Outlook* and poets I encountered, as will our readers, for the first time. Above all, I'm grateful to the poets whose work can be found in these pages. Every one of them has taught me something both about the art of poetry and about the inexhaustible richness of the classics.

July 2024

Rachel Hadas is the author of numerous collections of poems and essays and recently retired from Rutgers University-Newark, where she was Board of Governors Professor of English. She has translated Euripides's Iphigenia plays and a book of the *Dionysiaca of Nonnus*, published in 2022 as *Tales of Dionysus*. Her most recent books are essays, *Piece by Piece*, and poetry, *Pandemic Almanac* and *Ghost Guest*. *Forty-four Pastorals* is forthcoming. For more, see www.rachelhadas.net.

POETRY AND POSTLUDES

JORDI ALONSO

γῆρας προσδέχου

Some say the best thing that can happen is
never to be born into the world
and so avoid each sunset to be seen
by our misfortuned eyes beyond the range
of mountains to the west and by the sea
of Aigeus. If you are hearing this
or reading it (half-misremembered) on some scroll
yourself, it is too late; you are alive.
Enjoy yourself. Thank Gaia for the trees
that give both shade and olives in return
for soul and sun. *Embrace old age* when nymphs
whose trees you planted when your teeth
fell out the first time care for you and yours.
Not everyone dies both renowned and young.

"γῆρας προσδέχου" is number 113 of 147 blank verse sonnets in a manuscript of mine, each based on one of the Delphic Maxims as reported by the fifth-century CE traveler Johannes Stobaeus in his *Anthologia*. These maxims, which sources tell us were either inscribed or somehow set up at the temple of Apollo at Delphi, were variously attributed in antiquity to priestesses, to the Seven Sages, or to Apollo himself. In this project, I have made them part of the poetic prophecies spoken by Themistoklea, a historical Pythia, or Priestess of Apollo, who lived in the sixth century BCE and was said to have been Pythagoras's teacher. Each of the sonnets translates its title (set off in italics from the rest of the text) somewhere in the body of the poem. It is not my purpose to explicate the poem here, but rather to sketch a craft note that might explain some of my thinking for the entire manuscript. I wrote these sonnets in part while I was studying nymph cults at Columbia University. Wilamowitz famously said in a lecture at Oxford "if you wish to make the ancients speak, you must feed them with your own blood." I skinned my knees in May of 2022 a few meters from the Propylaea because my eyes were lifted up to the architecture of the Acropolis, and, like Socrates in Aristophanes's *Clouds*, I was walking on the air.

I have been studying nymphs and nymph cults since my days as an undergraduate at Kenyon College. My MA thesis at Columbia focused on nymphs in the Orphic Hymns, and my dissertation at the University of Missouri was on the reception of nymphs in Victorian literature. Naturally, my nympholepsy has manifested creatively as well. Since my source for the Delphic Maxims is Stobaeus, I gathered other tidbits from the *Anthologia* to include in the poems as well. The first three lines of 113 are a metrical translation of various sources – a proverb variously attributed to Aristotle (via Plutarch, *Moralia* 115a-c), *The Contest of Homer and Hesiod*, Theognis (425-28), and many others.

I'm particularly interested (creatively and otherwise, at the moment) in prophecy and speech acts by nymphs. In the Orphic Hymn to the Nereids, the speaker of the poem tells us that the Nymphs first revealed the mystic rites which are part of Orphic cult to the initiates who are, at that moment, participants in the cult of Orpheus. The prophecies of the prophet-poet Bakis, an ancient Nostradamus-like figure, were also said to have been inspired by the Nymphs. Collecting the fragments of Bakis scattered across extant Greek literature has been a goal of mine for about a year, but I digress. The final source of my sonnet is Thetis's famous reported prophecy by Achilles, who, in *Iliad* 9.410-15, says his mother told him his life would play out in one of two ways if he went to Troy. Let us, then, all hope for κλέος, not through acts of heroic valor, but through quiet stewardship of the world. After you read this issue, plant native flowers in your yard, leave water out for the bees, and when you take something from nature, thank the Nymphs for providing it, and remind them of how you've used their previous gifts.

Jordi Alonso holds an AB in English from Kenyon College, an MA in Classical Studies from Columbia University, and a Ph.D. in Victorian Literature and Creative Writing from the University of Missouri. He is the author of the poetry collections *Honeyvoiced* and *The Lovers' Phrasebook*. His work has appeared in *The Kenyon Review*, *The Southampton Review*, and elsewhere. He is working on three projects involving the eighteenth-century Jesuit Latin poet, Ubertino Carrara; the reception of Greek texts in the Renaissance; and the reception of classical ruins in nineteenth-century Anglophone poetry. He currently teaches at Louisiana State University.

CATHERINE ANDERSON

Diana's Arrow

How often do I avoid the truth
even as it arrows my way,

sleek & unsubtle. Last summer
the city abandoned the public pool

I loved with its flowered filigree facing
Cedar Road, built before cities rose up

to spark their necessary fires, built when
a Black child who wanted to swim here

would have been barred from entering.
But that was the past, I told myself.

For months I watched the pool fade
away with the finches & lilac trees

until it turned stagnant, pigeon feathers
scumming the tiles. Whatever injustice

occurred long ago can't happen again,
I told myself. Nearby, I saw oak leaves

had settled like a helmet of ash on a statue
of Diana – protector of children,

women, all living things – the deity
whose arrow never misses.

You'd think she might have tired
of the chase, that she'd had

enough of human evasion, yet plucked
from her heavy quiver I could see

another arrow, one she would send to arc
the sky & pierce my heart until I got it.

 Goddess of the hunt, Diana was revered by the Romans as the protector of living creatures, including mothers, children, animals, enslaved people, and young men. The sight of the ancient goddess, quiver at her side, arrow drawn, in a contemporary space serves as a bridge from ancient times to modern day when conflicts of power continue to encroach upon vulnerable lives. It may be hard to think of this lovely goddess as a sharpshooter, but here she is aiming for the speaker's naïve belief that racial injustice is a thing of the past. Working through the draft, I looked back at Edith Hamilton's *Mythology*, where she describes a deity not only tender and protective but also aggressive. If figures from mythology and what they do are aspects of our consciousness, then, in this poem, Diana's arrow is the beginning of doubt, sent flying to question our presumptions.

 Less than ten years ago I remember that many of us working in nonprofits committed to anti-poverty work thought those who held racist beliefs would naturally die off and their ideas fade away. How wrong we were. In the neighborhood where I live is an old park set among trees and a swing set with nearby statues of two protecting gods. The park had been named for someone whose racist views were once either tolerated or ignored. Only recently did the board overseeing the park finally, with reluctance, change the name. I am always startled by how long it takes us to realize a hard truth about our own culture. Reading the myths is one way to experience, however late, those hidden arrows of consciousness.

Catherine Anderson's most recent book is a memoir, *My Brother Speaks in Dreams: Of Family, Beauty & Belonging* (Wising Up Press). A contributor to the group translation of *Tales of Dionysus: The Dionysiaca of Nonnus of Panopolis*, she has also published four collections of poetry and has received awards from the Massachusetts Artists' Foundation, the *I-70 Review* and the *Crab Orchard Review*. She lives in Kansas City, MO, where she works with spoken-language interpreters in the city's immigrant communities.

JOSEPHINE BALMER

The funerary inscription of a three-year-old child, Publius Aurarius Crescens, from the University of Birmingham Archaeology Collection (provenance and date unknown) © pending Research and Cultural Collections, University of Birmingham, on loan from Birmingham Museums Trust. (Copyright permission was granted when *CO* 99.3 was published in the fall of 2024.)

A Different Growth

(Child's funerary inscription, Rome, date unknown)

By then we knew we had to count.

He'd woken in the night, cried a little,
so I rubbed his swollen stomach;
I stayed to watch him breathe, in and out,
his shrivelled arms like reed stems, brittle
to the touch, his skin blanched papyrus.
The most loved son, the most dutiful,
Crescens: three years, seven months, eight days . . .
We'd named him for vigour, for strength.
Until they told us: he had a different growth.

That morning his sickle moon was etched
above the sky as if it could not bear to set.
As if time had slowed. Stopped. Like the sliver
of splintered heart now lodged in my throat.

Every November, the UK Being Human Festival sees universities across the country partner with creative practitioners and local community groups to offer a program of events celebrating the arts and humanities. Last year, with a theme of "Rhyme or Reason," I was invited by Dr. Elena Theodorakopoulos of the University of Birmingham to write a group of poems inspired by its small but perfectly-formed classics and archaeology museum collection.

Among the collection's many beautiful treasures, I came across a small, modest Latin inscription, an epitaph for a very young boy, Publius Aurarius Crescens, set up by his "most unhappy parents," Aurarius Trophimus and Vibia Frontis. At once I was taken by the incredibly precise – and heart-breaking – detail the inscription gives of Crescens's short time on earth. I was also struck by the meaning of his name which in Latin means something that thrives or grows but also something that swells or becomes enlarged.

In this way, my poem began to take shape. I decided to voice it through Crescens's mother, Vibia, in order to give speech to the more often silent women of Rome. But this also had a deeply personal resonance as my sister's young daughter had died of a childhood cancer many years before.

I later learned from the collection's curator, Dr. Maeve McHugh, that the authenticity of this particular piece is in doubt; although the inscription itself is known from Rome (*CIL* 6.12957), the original has long been lost. It appears that the Birmingham artifact is probably a copy, if carved on a piece of ancient marble, and perhaps made for the Grand Tour souvenir market. But to me, this doesn't diminish its power or significance, which are only increased by the way it has spoken to us across all the centuries.

Josephine Balmer's most recent collection is *Ghost Passage* (2022). Her previous collection, *The Paths of Survival*, was short-listed for the 2017 London Hellenic Prize and was a Poetry Book of the Year in *The Times*. Other collections include *Letting Go: Thirty Mourning Sonnets* (2017), *The Word for Sorrow* (2009), and *Chasing Catullus: Poems, Translations & Transgressions* (2004). She has also published the translations *Catullus: Poems of Love and Hate* (2004), *Classical Women Poets* (1996), and *Sappho: Poems and Fragments* (1992).

AL BASILE

A Pig's Eye

She understood me better than she knew.
Once the emptied bowls slipped from our grasp
and dully clanged against the polished stone
beneath our feet, her hospitality

revealed its true intent. As bristles sprouted
out on our bodies' every inch, we fell
grunting in a bunch on hands and knees
and snuffled at the fragrant table legs.

She led us out a back way to the sties,
our bellies dragging in the luscious mud,
with men's minds still, trapped in a herd of swine.
My shipmates squealed in protest at their fate.

I, though, was thinking it a stroke of luck.
Our voyage had been one calamity

after another. Blown across the sea,
skulls cracked between the one-eyed Giant's jaws

or beaten flat by rocks heaved from above,
we felt like playthings in a children's game.
It turned out our captain was a hero.
You want to stay away from gods and heroes.

The captain was tipped off about the spell –
this god or that was always helping him,
it seemed – so he could make the sorceress
explain the only way he could get home.

That was his motivation, getting home.
Of course, he had a kingdom, and a queen
waiting for him. He was in a hurry.
I don't blame him – if I had a home

and someone to go back to, I'd be, too.
But there was nothing for me where I'd started.
I'd signed on to the mission on a lark,
to get away. Who knew that it was doomed?

So when she changed us back, I thought about
the life that we'd be starting up again.
I couldn't help comparing it to what
I had – slop buckets kept full to the brim,

free foraging the island roots and acorns,
the cool wet mud where I could sink my toes;
a life without demands or incident.
And silently, alone, I cursed the outcome.

Oh, to be men again! my shipmates snorted,
cheered by the chance to sleep next to their oars
below decks, quarters cramped on every side,
to bristle at an order, but obey.

I hung back once the changing had begun,
and watched them wash themselves, their bodies smooth,
and put on clothes to hide their nakedness.
They'd all agree again to get along,

and die trying. When the spell began
to wear off in me, I could feel the urge
to stand up on two feet. I sniffled then;
a tear rolled from my eye, dropped from my snout.

"A Pig's Eye" is a meditation on the quality of life and attitude in both the ancient and the modern world. Told in the voice of one of Odysseus's crewmen, it comments on life as a pig under Circe's spell – before, during, and after, concluding with the transformation back to human. The speaker is one of the anonymous crew members – not given a name or backstory in the epic itself – and reminds us that their lives were swept along with that of Odysseus without their knowledge or approval. As the saying goes, just as when elephants fight, the ants tremble. When heroes meet their fate, their companions are forced to suffer with it.

The twist on the treatment is that such a man might well prefer life as a pig to the one he'd endured as an expendable member of Odysseus's crew. He says he joined the adventure "on a lark" and that his life was not in any way privileged; unlike the hero, he had nothing to go back to. So for him, the life of a pig was a form of classless freedom he found preferable. Unlike him, his shipmates were all happy to be turned back into men. The language of the poem leads us through his impressions during the transformation by using physical detail from his point of view, ending with his urge to stand on two feet again, but having a tear drop from his snout – suggesting that there is a crossfade in his consciousness and a progression in his changing sense of identity.

The larger subject of the poem is the relative situation of nameless people in the modern world, who might also prefer a life of simple needs met without the burden of moral decisions: a life without responsibility. In this way, the poem gives voice to the struggle to cope with the demands of being human, in any era. It also implies that justice and injustice in our lives are related to the choices we make – whether we consider the implications of those choices or not at the time.

Al Basile, poet/playwright, singer/songwriter, and cornetist, is known to blues fans worldwide, with twenty solo albums and eight nominations for Blues Music Awards. He has three books of poetry and five verse audio plays. His 2022 play, *Open Question*, won a platinum award from the HEARnow national audio drama festival. He is a member of the Powow River poets and has taught at the West Chester Poetry Conference. He is the host of the online poets-in-conversation show, *Poems On*.

Two Poems

MEREDITH BERGMANN

The Roman Portraits

This part of the museum isn't lit.
These galleries contain sarcophagi
consuming loves I left unconsummated.
I made no likenesses of them, alive,
and have no narrative to carve along
their narrow flanks: no godlike play, no flight
from rape, no next seduction. Their remains,
lacking wall texts, must lie here unremembered,
including marble heads of men who looked

right at me, woke me, marking my arousal.
My sexiest professor's here, in profile,
as in his car after the circus. So strong,
he didn't turn to look at me that night.
I fled. The empire fell. This week, he's dead.

I've been writing a series of retrospective sonnets about my sentimental education, set in an imaginary museum. When I first visited the National Archaeological Museum in Naples in 1994, it was grimy and staffed only by grouchy old men, and many of the treasures taken from Pompeii were invisible because the lights were simply out in various galleries. Parts of my life have felt like that – as a young woman I spent much of my time trying to understand who I was to men.

As a sculptor, I've considered the Metropolitan Museum my second home. Many of my sculptures have been inspired by studying, emulating, and even purposefully misunderstanding the Met's collection of archaic torsos, Roman funerary altars, and portrait heads. So much of Grecian grace and Roman authority feels beyond my reach as an artist, but I continue to study. I find the specificity of Roman portrait sculpture very moving, especially when the name of the subject is lost and we are left only with the way their character and experience have shaped their features. A *Male Portrait* in marble may have a provocative lean and hungry look, or, at the other end of some spectrum of power, alarmingly sagging cheeks and a weary, furrowed brow. But they convince us that they lived, and in ways recognizable to us.

Roman sarcophagi (the word means "flesh-eating") seemed the right place to store fading memories of men I never got to know, or ran away from before I could turn into a creature in which I could not recognize myself.

Psyche Revisits the Closet of Venus

She gave me cast-offs I was glad to wear
because they were so rich and beautiful,
although they didn't complement my hair
or skin tone. I was young and dutiful

and dazzled by her luxury and taste,
her make-up, scent and jewels. I wore work clothes.
She'd twist embroidered sashes round her waist
over tight girdles: poetry, not prose.

She'd make me watch her dress. "Do I look fat?"
What could I say? She wasn't young, or slim,
but saw herself as an aristocrat.
I kept my falsehoods simple, sweet and prim.

What could I give a queen whose wardrobe's full,
who owned so much Chanel and Givenchy?
I knit a suit of delicate gold wool
from rare Greek goats, which she sent back to me

for alterations, many times. I made
a purse for her from seed pearls, and she said
my hands were clever. Are my debts not paid?
And who will wear these clothes when she is dead?

This poem is the second in a series of eight I'm calling *Psyche in Connecticut*. My complicated and frustrating forty-year relationship with my mother-in-law decayed rapidly after we moved into a house in Connecticut with her in her final years. I began to write about my various attempts to win her respect and love, and I looked to classical literature for a way to aggrandize my struggles so much that I would then be able to find their absurdity, to see how ridiculous it was to feel so wounded for so long, to "let it go." I asked a friend, the wonderful poet and classicist A. E. Stallings, to recommend a nightmarish mother-in-law from classical literature and she suggested Apuleius's Venus in the story of Cupid and Psyche from *The Golden Ass*.

What a trove! I delighted in the story's humor and viciousness and absurdity – all recognizable from this relationship! I loved finding the origins of Rumpelstiltskin and Cinderella in Apuleius. Thinking back over the many odd jobs my mother-in-law hired me to do when I was young, restoring her antiques and carpets, running errands to buy fabric of just the right color and, later, shopping all over Manhattan for narrowly specific foods and drinks, it was easy to feel the parallels with the punishing labors forced on Psyche by Venus, and to create a speaker of the poems who feels bewildered and misused.

My mother-in-law was willing to spend freely on herself and on beautiful things to live among, all of which my husband and I have inherited. I would rather try to make beautiful things, and I made her many gifts over the years. The gold wool for knitting comes directly from Book Six and its shining sheep. The purse of seed pearls is a combination of the heap of seeds Psyche must sort and some of the oceanic attributes of Venus with which my poems are salted. I'm very grateful to Alicia Stallings and Apuleius for lending me the freedom to revel in my characters' resentment, aggression, foolishness, and spite. And I do wear some of her things.

Meredith Bergmann is an award-winning sculptor. Her *Women's Rights Pioneers Monument* was unveiled in Central Park in August 2020, and she has just unveiled a monument for the historic center of Lexington, MA. Her poetry has appeared in many journals and anthologies. Her chapbook, *A Special Education*, was published in 2014 by EXOT Books, and an illustrated poetry book, *The Dying Flush*, was published by EXOT in 2024. Pictures of her work may be seen at www.meredithbergmann.com.

ELIJAH PERSEUS BLUMOV

A Bottle (According to Aristotle)

Hule
The sea vents lunar wrath upon the earth,
and sand ensues. Stolen, fired, blown
with breath, and glass is given violent birth.

Eidos
Once, before mankind was fully grown,
a clever ape reckoned that it could pour
the river into something it could own.

Kinoun
The grim Venetian makes the flames to roar,
and churns the emerald syrup into craft.
He sweats, and sighs – he only has five more.

Telos
It's made to hold a thing that makes us daft –
why hoard such vicious poison willingly?
So we might say: we wept less than we laughed.

The note is tucked inside – and, filled with glee,
the children toss the bottle back to sea.

The terza rima sonnet is one of my favorite forms. Not only does it possess inherent beauty and rigor and a Dantesque aura, but it encourages the sonnet to do something it doesn't normally do: namely, tell a story. Compared to an octave and a sestet (an Italian sonnet), or three quatrains and a couplet (an English sonnet), the terza rima arrangement feels so much more capacious: you have a generous four tercets in which to develop a theme or narrative, and then, on top of that, an opportunity to offer a snappy flourish or judgment upon the preceding events in the concluding couplet.

It struck me that the quadripartite structure of this type of sonnet (excluding the couplet) would lend itself well to a meditation on one of the famous conceptual quartets: the four seasons, the four elements, the four cardinal virtues, etc. The trick, however, was to avoid subjects that I felt would be too cliched, didactic, or unsurprising. It was then that my love of Aristotle came to my rescue, and I had it – I would write a poem on the four Aristotelian causes.

In Aristotle's thought, one can respond to the question, "why does x object exist?" in four ways. Firstly, one can give an account of what material(s) the thing is made of: this is its material cause (ὕλη / *hūlē*). Secondly, one can give an account of the design according to which the thing was constructed: this is its formal cause (εἶδος / *eîdos*). Thirdly, one can give an account of what agent or source produced the thing: this is its efficient cause (κινοῦν / *kinoûn*), and this is typically what people mean by "cause" in modern speech. Finally, one can give an account of what purpose the object was created to fulfill: this is its final cause (τέλος / *télos*). Someone who possesses knowledge of each of the four causes in relation to a given object has a comprehensive answer for why the given object exists.

I thought it might be fun to illustrate the idea of the four causes in a poem by using a particular object as a case study. Very often, a poem about an object is devoted to probing the depths of that object's significance. What better way, I thought, to examine an object from all angles than to meditate upon its four causes in sequence? Such was the teleological cause of the poem before you. As for the couplet, I wanted it to address a cause (or two) undreamt of in Aristotle's philosophy.

Elijah Perseus Blumov is a poet and the host of the poetry analysis podcast, *Versecraft*. His poetry has been published or is forthcoming in periodicals such as *Literary Matters*, *Birmingham Poetry Review*, *The Alabama Literary Review*, and *Think Journal*. He lives in Chicago.

DAVID CAPPS

When Icarus Fell

He did not cry out. His father was too far ahead,
even when they stood together in the tower in Crete
looking out at the chasm between their two fates,

Daedalus was too far ahead to hear him. Icarus knew
he would fail, and not the wings his father fashioned
and affixed with wax. They seemed to buffer every

possible updraft, like a pair of swanlike arguments
smoothed in his hands, a rebuttal for each reply.
Dust motes danced in the prison of their golden rays,

slowly intending an end. Icarus knew he would fail,
despite his father's cautioning not to fly too close
to the sun, nor too close to the sea. What did it mean,

"too far," "too close"? He lacked his father's arete.
There were times he stumbled in his speech, wanting
to put into words what was already fully formed.

He would shrug, cast up his eyes, and nod in silence.
Had his passive resignation been born of piety instead
of forbearance, would it have been any less tragic?

This poem has its origins in my travels both to Crete and Ikaria in recent years. When I was in Ikaria, I read every poetic treatment of the myth I could find. Among the most poignant to me was the poem "Daedalus" by modernist Greek poet Angelos Sikelianos. Sikelianos treats Daedalus as a symbol of invention and transcendence, and the fall of Icarus is presented less as a tragedy and more as a sign of inevitable human progress. To facilitate his ideal and make it real for the reader, Sikelianos launches into the entire scene and characterization of the fall.

When I began, I wanted to focus on the fall itself, and so I wrote a very different poem that attempts to single out the sense of vertigo experienced both in terms of the physical fall, how the actual cliffs of Ikaria seem to fall into the sea, and the psychological sense of the fallen: fallen youth, fallen civilization, fallen aspirations, shame. At the same time, most poets who've approached the topic labor in the shadow of Bruegel's painting and its ekphrastic treatments, which I have explored in my essay "Icarus, Icarus" (*The Antonym* 2021).

One central idea reflected in the treatments of William Carlos Williams and W. S. Merwin is that tragedies occur on a daily basis, and go unnoticed until we choose to call attention to them. This influence, I think, led me to write a very different sort of poem than the initial inspiration, one that focused more on the interior thought processes of an Icarus destined to fail/fall but who has full knowledge of that fact.

Given my background in philosophy and interest in virtue ethics, I also began to think about moral questions concerning the fall of Icarus. Mightn't our moral evaluation of this hypothetical event depend on the system of values assumed, whether Ancient Greek or Christian? If the father were a famous somebody and the son living in his shadow, how might Icarus internalize the felt absence of self-worth without emerging as a pathetic figure? I suppose each of these ideas helped to give the poem its traction.

David Capps is a philosophy professor and poet who lives in New Haven, CT. He is the author of four chapbooks: *Poems from the First Voyage* (The Nasiona Press, 2019), *A Non-Grecian Non-Urn* (Yavanika Press, 2019), *Colossi* (Kelsay Books, 2020), and *Wheatfield with a Reaper* (Akinoga Press, forthcoming). His latest work, *On the Great Duration of Life,* a riff on Seneca's *On the Shortness of Life,* is available from Schism Neuronics.

CHRISTOPHER CHILDERS

Aristotle at Pyrrha

All men by nature seek knowledge. – Aristotle

  It's the eyes I remember – they took in
everything. Always looking. No one knew
where he came from, but one day there he was,
walking the docks and clambering in our sloops,
inspecting everything our nets hauled in.
  At first, he hardly talked, just concentrated,
but sometimes asked odd questions, all about
the seasons and the movements of the fishes,
when we catch what, and where. It's not clear why
we answered him. We griped about the pesky
starfish, and how a drought did in the clams;
we said the fish leave the lagoon in winter,
all but the gudgeons, and – he thought this strange –
sea-urchins here taste best in wintertime,
when they're all full of eggs. We said that once
we had a wounded dolphin on the boat,
and the pack swarmed us till we let it go,
and then swam off. And we explained the use
of pickles in the eel-traps, how the smell
attracts them, and we took him through the marsh
where the perch-eggs are wrapped around the reeds
like fishing line, and showed him how to dredge
the bottom to dislodge the fattest sprats,
and how to salt the fry to make them keep.
He wrote it down. He wrote down everything.
  He had a knife. He went around with it
and slit things open: Chicken eggs and insects
(an insect lives a long time cut in half,
he told us) and chameleons, tortoises

(their legs keep wiggling when the heart is out)
and eels and cuttlefish. He loved them best,
the cuttlefish, their colors and their cunning.
He opened them and looked at everything.
And shellfish, shellfish, shellfish. Maybe so,
I said, but they're delicious! No reaction.
He wasn't one for jokes. His Greek was funny.
Like comes from like, he'd say, unlike from unlike.
We nodded as if he was making sense.

   At night, we talked around the fire. We said
that we'd caught fish like sticks, of uniform
thickness, black and round. And we had seen
creatures like shields, deep crimson, dense with fins,
billowing on the waves, and other creatures
like penises, with fins where testicles
should be; somebody caught one on a nightline.
We told how Chians had shipped oysters in
and raised them in the straits, where the tides clash;
they didn't reproduce, but sure got big!
Of course he wrote that down. And he talked too.
He told us animals that copulate
have parents like themselves, but animals
that don't, because they lack the organs or
the differences of gender, just appear
spontaneously out of different species,
or from a mix of rain and rotten matter:
The sweet rain makes the animals, the rotten
matter is residue. He said it happens
chiefly in the heat, which causes ferment,
and makes things bubble up. He said that sperm
is white because it's hot and full of bubbles.
It sounded crazy, yet somehow made sense.

   He wasn't done. He said that everything
has god in it, that animals are divine,
that souls aren't in our bodies, that although
they make us move, they never move themselves,
and that makes them like god, the souls that is,
because he sits alone outside the world
and thinks it into being, all of us
his thoughts, like bubbles, little fillips of foam
winking up out of the ocean of his mind,
and that what matters is to know his mind,

since god's mind is the soul of the whole world;
and all things living, even plants, have souls,
and when the body dies, the soul dies with it.
He could have started up his own religion!
Somebody would have followed it. He said
eels are the spawn of earthworms in the mudflats,
and flies spring on their own from rotting meat,
and mites from wax, mullets from mud and sand,
sponges and crabs and oysters come from slime,
and mussels send out shoots and bud like onions,
and that the queen bee, uninseminated
herself, gives virgin birth to the whole tribe,
and snails make love, but nothing comes of it.
He said in the Crimea there's a river,
Hypanis, that around the summer solstice
rolls in its current little sacks like grapes,
and when each bursts this winged quadruped
flies out, and flies till evening, when it dies.
And he said there's a fish born out of foam
when rain from heaven makes the ocean sweet;
a sort of sprat, that twinkles on the rollers
like silver coins. He said that everywhere
is god, and all we have to do is look.
   At the end we would stand there watching him
as he moved solitary through the marshes
and meadows, hunkering down to flowers, or scrabbling
under the dock for barnacles and sea-squirts,
or pacing the whole length of the lagoon,
bending and touching things. After a while,
seemed like the animals would come to him,
the tortoises, cicadas and chameleons,
offering themselves, impatient to be known.
We watched him looking out on the lagoon,
standing on a rock, just quiet, thinking,
his shadow lengthening atop the waves
backlit by the sunset, lengthening
over the glassy, unreflecting waves,
over the wave-tops and the centuries,
dark on the shimmer, human-shaped and not.
Catch the light just right and you can see it
still, if you look. And us, we're all still here,
walking the docks and taking out our sloops,

casting our nets and hauling in the catch,
filleting fish, and throwing out the guts,
but him? We never saw another one
like him, and I don't guess we ever will.

"Aristotle at Pyrrha" came out of a series of three History of Science lectures I attended during graduate school on the theme of "spontaneous generation." This is the idea that some types of animals, like fleas, maggots, and eels, are generated *sponte sua*, without mating or reproducing, from nonliving matter. Aristotle is the earliest major proponent of the theory; the poem shows him during his two-year sojourn on Lesbos, examining the wildlife of the island for his works on natural science. (An enjoyable recent book on this subject is *The Lagoon* by Armand Leroi Marie.) Initially I had hoped to write other poems about spontaneous generation, focusing on such proto-scientists as Albertus Magnus and Athanasius Kircher, and still might, if I can ever find the energy. In general, I'm interested in discredited theories not because their exponents were stupid (quite the opposite, obviously), but because it is so easy to dismiss the past without reflecting that we are just as likely to be dismissed by the future. I guess it was from a sense of humility about the limits of knowledge that the poem was (not quite spontaneously) generated.

Christopher Childers is the author of *The Penguin Book of Greek and Latin Lyric Verse,* published in 2024 by Penguin Classics. His work has appeared in various journals, including *Literary Matters*, *The Kenyon Review*, *The Yale Review*, *The Hopkins Review*, and *Smartish Pace*. He is a recent transplant to Los Angeles, CA, where he lives with his wife and teaches Latin.

TERESE COE

This Is No Longer Troy

Hecuba speaks to Polyxena, murdered:
the daughter who promised herself to Achilles
in a failed attempt to save Troy.

Odysseus came to Troy to spy, my child.
Crusted with dirt, blood running down his face,
he fell at my feet and implored me for help.

When I claimed a return of the favor
I had bestowed, I begged the wily one
to end this war.

All wasted idly on the air.

I saw a red doe torn from my knees,
mangled by a wolf with bloodied fangs.
Still warm and youthful, dead.

What songs have been sung in praise of daughters?
None. What could they possibly have to say?
A girl
lies here
whom the Greeks
have feared
and killed?

Not you are here to comfort me,
child, but I,
childless, aged, homeless,
must cover you in earth,
my darling girl,
my youngest daughter,
Polyxena.

I discovered my first Greek drama, *The Trojan Women*, while babysitting for my cousin as a young teen and browsing through my aunt and uncle's bookshelves. I took that volume down because "Trojan" and "Women" were in the title. Especially "Women." I had no idea what I was in for.

I had read the *Odyssey* but not yet the *Iliad*. Later, after I'd seen Greek drama performed, the drama became more transformative and memorable to me than any literature I knew; the historical qualities and Chorus excited me. Greek tragedy filled me with admiration and affection for first Athena and later Artemis; each one was a *genius loci* for me, a private influencer. Of course, one couldn't easily speak about Greek goddesses as conscious advisers in the era before, say, 1970 and the renewed feminist movement. But now and then I did.

For a college German course I read Goethe's *Iphigenie auf Tauris* (1779). In it Agamemnon's missing eldest daughter has not been sacrificed or killed by the Greeks but escapes and lives as a priestess of Artemis on an island, Taurica, where Orestes finds her. As an eldest daughter I felt that play too was a gift that expanded upon information I needed.

About the courage and independence of Artemis and Iphigenia: It's one thing to empathize with a Jane Eyre or an Elizabeth Bennet or another female protagonist in an English novel, but an entirely more austere and motivating matter to identify with Andromache, Cassandra, Hecuba, Iphigenia, or Polyxena. When my formal education was behind me, I once came awfully close to being murdered by attackers, would-be rapists, in a forest in Alsace, and I fought long enough to be rescued by complete strangers who came upon the scene. The rescuers brought me to the police, who brought me to a local hospital for an overnight examination. Every one of my possessions had been stolen by the perps. When I asked for pen and notepaper to write my family in New York (this was years before the internet), a nun-nurse in a white cap with outstretched "wings" brought me a pad of writing paper. On the cover was a beautiful embossed white image of Artemis on a sky-blue background, running through the Greek forest, alone, drawing an arrow from her quiver.

I can't say precisely how writing "This is No Longer Troy" has been influenced by a sense-memory of Polyxena's murder, but perhaps the poem will suggest an answer.

Terese Coe's poems, translations, and prose appear in over one hundred journals internationally, including *Agenda, Alaska Quarterly, Cincinnati Review, Cyphers, Hopkins Review, Metamorphoses, The Moth, New American Writing, Ploughshares, Poetry, Poetry Review, Stinging Fly, Threepenny Review*, and the *TLS*. Two of her books of poems are *The Everyday Uncommon* (2005) and *Shot Silk* (2015). Her black comedy, *Harry Smith at the Chelsea Hotel*, was read at Dixon Place, SRO, by Equity Actors in 2019. Please see https://en.wikipedia.org/wiki/Terese_Coe.

ARMAND D'ANGOUR

After "Atys": Channelling A. E. Housman

In Greek mythology (as recounted by Plutarch, Pausanias, and others) Aegeus, the aged king of Athens, awaited the return of his son Theseus from Crete, whence the hero had set out to kill the monstrous Minotaur. Aegeus had asked him to hoist white sails as news of success; black sails would mean his quest had failed and he was dead. Theseus forgot his father's request, and when Aegeus saw the black-sailed ship returning from Crete he cast himself into the sea in sorrow – hence giving it the name of the Aegean. The tragic tale inspired this poem, which is modelled closely (or pastiched) on "Atys" by A. E. Housman (1859-1936).

The Death of Aegeus

"Dwellers by Ilissus river
Tillers of Athena's loam:
See you now the sails a-quiver?
Theseus' ship returning home?"

"King, the star that shuts the even   5
Calls the sheep from Parnēs down;
Home return the doves from heaven,
And the prince to Pallas' town."

Hastening from their Cretan glory,
On the foam-flecked waves they cross;   10
Hoisted sails must tell their story:
White for triumph, black for loss.

"Drinkers of the nine-mouthed fountain,
You who mine the argent vein:
Comes he safe from Ida's mountain?   15
Shining sail-sheets see you plain?"

"King, my eyes are not unerring:
Still the sails are scarce in sight;
Far I see a shadow stirring;
That I spy. I spy not white."   20

"Look once more, your head inclining
(It is eve and I am old)
Tell me Theseus' sails are shining
White, more precious far than gold;

> I am old, and day is ending, 25
> And the darkening night falls fast;
> Up to Sounion's cliffs now wending
> Spy you not white sails at last?"
>
> Loud the land with sounds of mourning.
> Cold the body from the waves. 30
> Home is nigh, and day is dawning:
> Proud the hero comes who saves.

NOTES

1 **Ilissus**: the river that runs through Athens. 2 **Athena's loam**: the earth of Athens, whose patron goddess was Athena 5 **shuts the even** (Housman's phrase) means "ends the evening" 6 **Parnēs**: one of the central hills of Athens 8 **Pallas**: another name for Athena 13 **nine-mouthed fountain**: a feature of ancient Athens, the *Enneakrounos* ("nine-fountain") spring 14 **argent vein**: silver mines in Athens's territory enriched the city; the fact that this was a later find (early fifth century) makes this a conscious anachronism 15 **Ida**: the highest mountain in Crete 27 **Sounion**: the southernmost cape of Athens.

Housman's "Atys" is based on the tragic story told in the *Histories* of Herodotus (1.35-45), which tells of Atys the son of Croesus, king of Lydia. Croesus dreamed that Atys would be killed by a spear, so to forestall this coming to pass he refused to send him out to fight in battle. When a monstrous boar began to terrorize the land of Mysia, its people appealed to Croesus for help, and Atys persuaded his father to let him accompany a troupe of young men selected to drive away the boar, arguing that since boars do not wield spears he had nothing to fear. Croesus agreed and sent his house-guest Adrastus to guard his son from danger. During the hunt, Adrastus hurled his spear at the boar; it missed and killed Atys, as Croesus's dream had predicted.

Housman's rhythm and rhyme pack an emotional punch, as does his spare telling. The exchange between king and courtiers in *The Death of Aegeus* is framed exactly on that between the king and his courtiers in Housman's poem. Housman's most striking and brilliant device is to switch perspectives in the final stanza, from those awaiting the return of Atys to the dismal troupe bringing the boy's body home. It felt worth honouring Housman by creating a similar version for the story of Aegeus, but the heart-stopping tragedy and final bitter irony ("his father's pride") of the original poem is unsurpassed.

Atys
by A. E. Housman

'Lydians, lords of Hermus river,
Sifters of the golden loam,
See you yet the lances quiver
And the hunt returning home?'

'King, the star that shuts the even
Calls the sheep from Tmolus down;
Home return the doves from heaven,
And the prince to Sardis town.'

From the hunting heavy laden
Up the Mysian road they ride;
And the star that mates the maiden
Leads his son to Croesus' side.

'Lydians, under stream and fountain
Finders of the golden vein,
Riding from Olympus mountain,
Lydians, see you Atys plain?'

'King, I see the Phrygian stranger
And the guards in hunter's trim,
Saviours of thy son from danger;
Them I see. I see not him.'

'Lydians, as the troop advances,
– It is eve and I am old –
Tell me why they trail their lances,
Washers of the sands of gold.

'I am old and day is ending
And the wildering night comes on;
Up the Mysian entry wending,
Lydians, Lydians, what is yon?'

Hounds behind their master whining,
Huntsmen pacing dumb beside,
On his breast the boar-spear shining,
Home they bear his father's pride.

Armand D'Angour is a Professor of Classics at the University of Oxford and Fellow of Jesus College. He writes on the music, literature, and culture of ancient Greece and Rome, and has researched the sounds of ancient Greek music. He composes poetry in English, Greek, and Latin, and was commissioned to compose Pindaric odes in Greek for the Olympic Games in 2004 and 2012.

DAVID FRANKLIN

Achilles' Heel

Achilles came to Troy to fight for glory,
Young and fierce, flashing like his spear;
And he succeeded. From that ancient story
Resounds his name; the echo of a cheer.

No man in Troy came close, no man on Earth;
So deadly fast, beautiful and tall.
But death was stalking from his very birth,
And we recall his weakness first of all,

The heel; overlooked by his poor mother,
Who tried so hard to keep her son from harm,
She went beneath the earth to make him other
Than a man; to save him with a charm.

The waters of the Styx missed the heel
That Paris struck, to prove that humans feel.

Achilles, the greatest warrior in the Trojan War, was famous for his fighting brilliance and for his heel. His immortal mother Thetis wanted to protect her baby from harm, so she took him to the Underworld and plunged him into the River Styx, whose water made his body invulnerable. She did not notice that the water did not touch the heel which she held. As Achilles fought in the last days of the war, Paris shot a poisoned arrow which Apollo guided into his heel, and Achilles was proven mortal at last.

David Franklin studied classics at Oxford and has been teaching at Abingdon School in England since 2000. He has published translations of Sophocles's *Antigone* and Euripides's *Bacchae*, and he is currently working on a new translation of the *Aeneid*. He has written a number of poems on classical and other themes. He particularly enjoys finding a note of contemporary resonance in an ancient story or offering a new perspective on a familiar myth.

Two Poems

JULIA GRIFFIN

Liber Tertius Decimus

So this is how it feels was all he thought,
The sword already cooling in his hand.
Yes – (he addressed his ghosts). *You understand.*
And no one spoke. Those comrades who had fought
So long with him, his men, his Trojan band,

Kept staring at him, silent, till he caught
The words, *Son of the Goddess* . . . and that brought
Him back. "Prince Turnus – take him. Make it grand."
He gave the shield to someone, wiped his face,
Prayed privately to Jupiter – stood still,
Like victor's marble, rooted to the place,
His piety remastering his will:
And saw his Iulus (born the self-same day
As Hector's son) look down, and move away.

Briseis Weeps for Patroclus

So they returned the slave-girl to her master,
Followed by tripods, cauldrons, shining horses;
Women, and twice their weight in gold and silver.
Everyone then thanked God it all was over
(Even the famous Ajax felt like crying),
And drank each other's health in wine and water.

All except one. Pelides, by the water,
Wept for his rage, that easy ancient master.
Over the empty beaches birds were crying
Aiai with bloody breath; Poseidon's horses
Stumbled towards him moaning – tumbled over –
Bared in their fall a world of salt and silver.

And there his mother, with her throat of silver,
Sang with her sisters in the halls of water;
Mourning her son before his life was over –
Mourning too deep for mortal love to master;
Yet from the camp arose a wail of horses;
The thankful sound of silenced women crying.

Briseis took her place and led their crying.
They brought out crimson cloaks and ewers of silver;
Weeping, they washed Patroclus, lord of horses,
Honoring him with praise, with precious water,
Calling him dear protector, gentle master:
A slave's lament for kindness, over, over.

At last she gave the sign: they must give over;
Little's enough, she knew, with women's crying.
And now she breathed her comfort like a master,

Her voice an echo of his mother's silver,
As the sheer sky's reflected in deep water;
As the dark waves follow those soaring horses.

Penned in their stall, Achilles' magic horses
(Gifts from above; divinity left over)
Bided man's time on mash and mortal water.
Not long to wait. She heard the herald crying;
The sunlight bleached his arms from bronze to silver.
She crouched behind her husband-killer master:

Watching him play the master with his horses,
Watching him rub their silver hides all over
(Needful no doubt as crying into water.)

Both poems come out of teaching World Literature for many years. When I first taught the *Aeneid*, I was baffled by how to talk about the ending: its abruptness and the clash with *pietas* as we've seen it earlier in the poem. (Of course, it's true that Aeneas has become more savage in the last two books, but still this is a shock.) The poem ends, in fact, the way the *Iliad* begins – not the way it ends, which is in a mood of *pietas*: respect for a guest, for a suppliant; honor for the dead. Maffeo Vegio is certainly not the only person to have wanted a different kind of ending, of the kind that lay easily to hand: marriage with Lavinia, a big feast of reconciliation with the Rutulians. But, over time, I've come to see that Virgil's ending is a masterstroke. At last the beleaguered hero is alone. The gods have shaken hands and gone home; none of them cares about Turnus. Aeneas is free to act on impulse, on passion, on personal pain and rage, and he does it. The *Aeneid* is not revised, no, but Book 12 is already very long, and Virgil cannot have meant to write a Book 13 (meaningless number), so the probability is that he wanted that angry, jagged ending, and that it is part of the meaning of the poem. So my sonnet imagines the moment immediately after, when Turnus is dead and Aeneas must face what he has done. He has invaded, like Achilles; he is the stronger hero, the goddess's son, like Achilles; now he has done as Achilles did. In the end, they are not that different. And the Empire he fathers will not be smooth and painless either, whatever Anchises may predict.

"Briseis" also comes from teaching World Literature. I've always been so moved by the descriptions of the slave-women mourning for Patroclus: they mourn him because they are told to do it, and because it is their only opportunity to mourn for what they have really lost (Book 19). I wanted to pause on that moment, to hold it in a sort of suspension: sestinas do that, with their dreamy, shimmery repetitions. (Or at least they can be dreamy and shimmery.) And I'm fascinated by Achilles's horses and their strange, magical dignity.

Julia Griffin teaches Renaissance English Literature at Georgia Southern University. She has an MA from Cambridge in Classics and a DPhil (= Ph.D.) from Oxford in English. Her poems have appeared in *Light, Lighten Up Online, Better than Starbucks,* and some other magazines. In 2022, she was the winner of the two Kim Bridgford Memorial Sonnet awards.

KATIE HARTSOCK

A Calm Cassandra

So many on stage or screen
have screamed her eyes
into a foamy trance
or curled up fetally,
high-pitched. Why must
she be the horse at the bit
her master and murderer
want to ride, hysterical
in ways that whinny up
the worst Greek or Victorian
ideas of woman, uterus
wandering? I want a rock
of a priestess, who looks straight
from her robes into the abyss
and says, *I made you*. I want
a calm Cassandra, applying
lip gloss at a red light
by the bridge about to explode.
Who shifts gears into park
when the prophecy's coming on.
Who says, *You're looking at me
like I've just grown a second head
but I assure you, it's always been there.*
Who serves subpoenas, rakes the leaves,
ignores producers' advice
to raise her voice and fling her wine
into the face that especially
deserves it. A Cassandra
who runs the research vessel
sailing away from the smoky remains
of her city, and chucks the chum
from bucket into sea.
Who plunges in without a cage
because the great whites will not
come for her. Or because they will.

I like to watch adaptations of stories surrounding Troy, in films or theatrical productions, and one character's portrayal I often find frustrating is Cassandra's. When faced with the sheer scope of the destruction and violence (including against herself) she sees, actors usually play her over the top – shrieks, rolling eyes, faints – in a way that conjures stereotypes, from fifth-century BCE Athens to nineteenth-century CE Britain, of female hysteria. The longevity itself of this stereotype of women's excessive emotion and subsequent weakness is enough to make eyes roll. I remember feeling shocked but not surprised when I first learned that hysteria is from the Greek for uterus, *hystera*; even etymology shows how women have been defined and doomed by our very biology to be unreliable, out of control, helpless.

But Cassandra is so powerful. Powerful even when she cannot, by Apollo's curse, convince anyone of the truth of what she knows. She steals the show in Aeschylus's *Agamemnon*. My poem dreams of how a contemporary Cassandra could act her part. She often exemplifies women telling difficult stories, and that's why I want her to possess strength and resolve. I don't know how ancient male actors would have portrayed her, but in general I find contemporary actors' portrayals of her disappointing in how their very behavior creates a sense of unreliability (ultimately inappropriate for her status as a prophet) by invoking specters of female hysterics, or infantilization. One stage adaptation I saw years ago in Chicago had Cassandra clinging to a pink teddy bear as she screamed.

And yet this might not be the decision of the woman playing her! It might be the (male?) director or playwright's own inherited stereotypical ideas of how Cassandra should be. So one of my ideal readers for this poem would be an actor about to play Cassandra, who would like to "ignore the producers' advice." I think of Louise Glück's fascinating observation that "The secrets we choose to portray *lose* power over us."[1] Glück's remark challenges a popular assumption that we are in thrall to the dark difficult things we know, and to reveal them also reveals our subjection. But what if the telling actually, as Glück suggests, implies a kind of power over them? That's how it is for my Cassandra.

NOTE

[1] Louise Glück, *Proofs & Theories, Essays on Poetry* (1994) 34; emphasis mine.

Katie Hartsock's second poetry collection, *Wolf Trees* (Able Muse Press), was listed as one of Kirkus Review's best poetry books of 2023. Her work has recently appeared in journals such as *The Threepenny Review*, *Tupelo Quarterly*, *Image*, *Oxford Poetry*, *Beloit Poetry Journal*, *Plume*, and *RHINO*. She is an associate professor of English at Oakland University in Michigan.

ANDREW HUDGINS

A Plague of Our Own Making

When the public divined that they were out of favor,
they consecrated thousands of their children
and led them to the bronze statue of Cronus,
the god of harvest, for what are time and death
to Cronus and his short scythe but a harvest –
Cronus the child eater, devourer of his own get?

The statue's hands extended, both palms up,
sloped toward the fire. Each child was placed, bound,
on those metallic hands and slowly rolled
into a fire the populace deemed sacred,
sacrificed to lessen public suffering.

In an armed democracy where everyone
enjoys the power to forfeit anyone,
the least of us can confer unto Cronus
the dearest offering for the greatest good.

And so, convinced we are under attack
and with our children dying of our plagues,
we also sacrifice our heirs to Cronus,
if willy nilly in the current manner.

We have surrendered unto Cronus children
because an errant basketball escaped
into an armed and angry neighbor's yard,
because a fast-food meal was missing fries,
because they found a gun and shot themselves,
because they were born Asian, Black, or Jewish –
all sloppy oblations that the god
placidly accepts with tilted palms.
Cronus, god of death and harvest, grants
nothing in return as supplicants
stare at his hooded eyes expectantly,
bewildered that the killing of our children
has failed to ease the killing of our children.

Reading Bruce Chilton's *Abraham's Curse: The Roots of Violence in Judaism, Christianity, and Islam* (2008), I was arrested by his survey of child sacrifice in the ancient world. As an adolescent boy, I'd read about human sacrifice, fascinated by a horror safely relegated to the past. At least I hoped it was, as I sat in church, side-eyeing my father as the preacher extolled Abraham's willingness to kill his son Isaac at God's command. We were to understand that if it were God's will, filicide is a good thing. Though I got the point, I was dubious. But so great was my father's faith that I wasn't entirely sure he wouldn't kill me if so ordered, though I was pretty sure that if he did, the law and my father would not see eye to eye and that my murder would make the newspapers. In other words, while child sacrifice seemed like a dead issue in 1950s America, it didn't feel like an *entirely* dead issue.

Prompted by Chilton, I looked up Diodorus Siculus's description of infanticide in ancient Carthage. Seeing their enemies camped outside their walls, the Carthaginians looked inside their hearts and determined they needed to double down on child sacrifice to their Cronus, about which they had become sadly lax. A good many Carthaginians had been disinclined to part with their own children and had apparently purchased and raised children to offer in their stead. Pondering the Greek encampment outside their walls, the Carthaginians determined that Cronus took a dim view of the substitutes on offer. Diodorus describes the result: "In their zeal to make amends for their omission, they selected two hundred of the noblest children and sacrificed them publicly; and others who were under suspicion sacrificed themselves voluntarily, in number not less than three hundred. There was in their city a bronze image of Cronus, extending its hands, palms up and sloping toward the ground, so that each of the children when placed thereon rolled down and fell into a sort of gaping pit filled with fire" (*The Library of History* 20.14.5-6).

As I read this passage in the Loeb Classical Library edition, I was stewing with rage, horror, and grief over the school massacres in Uvalde, Texas, and, ninety miles from me, in Nashville, and others that I have forgotten. There are so many – so many that as of 2022 the number one cause of childhood and adolescent deaths in the United States is gunfire.[1] It was not difficult to equate the unbelievable horror of the ancient world to the unbelievable horror we live with now. What are those totally preventable deaths if not a modern analog to child sacrifice, a national calculation that easy access to the means to kill children is more valuable to us than children?

NOTE

[1] Goldstick, Jason E., Rebecca M. Cunningham, and Patrick M. Carter. "Current Causes of Death in Children and Adolescents in the United States." *The New England Review of Medicine* 386.20, April 20, 2022. (https://tinyurl.com/mr2vz4jd). Accessed 7/19/24.

Andrew Hudgins is Humanities Distinguished Professor of English Emeritus at The Ohio State University. He was a finalist for the Pulitzer Prize and the National Book Award, and he now lives in rural Tennessee with his wife Erin McGraw and two dogs.

DAX JOHNSON

The Shade of Heracles

The glories of immortality:
I count some days in lions, some in stables,
And fall through the arms of Theseus
Into the dark – into this slender sable

Web of history, where all my days of youth
Sound now like aged refrains – with just my deeds as proof.

In Pavese's *Dialogues with Leuco* (1947), Circe describes an immortal feeling of jealousy for mortals and our particularly fragile state. I chose Heracles as a representative to explore this feeling of uncertainty mainly for how multifaceted Heracles himself is; he is, over those years of trial, a mortal, a demigod, a shade in Hades, and a god in Olympus, and those competing aspects made his ghost a seemingly fitting speaker for this particular lament. His possessing of both great deeds in life and a real proximity to divinity endows even his ghost with the kind of vitality that allows for real pain.

I wanted to explore the idea of the deific figure made up of history, deed, and story: a figure of an eternal past, circling their own narratives and themes. And while this way of life would generally be a state of contentment, or perhaps the bliss of unchanging perfection, the somber nature of a dead shadow would recognize it as a kind of necessary pain, or as all that remains. Absent the joy of godhood but perfectly cognizant of all their immortality and understanding, there would be nothing left to an existence of this sort beyond an endless rumination on the acclaim that it has already won.

Dax Johnson is a poet interested in the interplay between the transgressive and the sublime. Currently in the process of obtaining a Master's Degree in NYU's XE program, he enjoys giallos, horticulture, the works of James Broughton, and Assyriology. Other works of his can be found in *Rigorous* and *Carte Blanche*.

LARRY JOHNSON

The Goddess Drusilla

Still taller than her brother, with sorrel hair,
Eye-catchingly accoutered when alive,
She wakened to teal Olympus, deified.
Worshipped on earth as *Panthea*, but in the guise
Of Aphrodite here, she caught fierce glares
From lesser deities; the greater ones
Weren't charmed by a jumped-up human's carnal taint –
Besides, the now-virulent lavender of her breasts
Clashed with her hair's pale sunset orange. Spurned,
She used her new-found godly powers to craze
Gaius – sent that self-proclaimed divine
A frenzy that would ensure his quickening end
So he might join her soon, and they could show
The other gods, those beings vastly bored
In their vain, endless lives, what death could do.

I first came across the name Caligula in an essay by Cotton Mather in eleventh-grade American literature and have been fascinated with this emperor and his controversial life ever since. Suetonius and some other Latin historians tell us that Caligula committed incest with all his sisters but that Drusilla was his favorite. After her death, which most sources tell us was from a fever, Caligula's grief was immoderate, and he had her deified, she being the first Roman woman to receive this honor. I prefer to think that Caligula and Drusilla were truly in love, and I wanted to show this affection being carried over into her awakening as a goddess in the teal-colored glory of Olympus. One would like to know more about what she was like as a person, and perhaps that will be dealt with in another poem. The historical novel *Caligula* by Douglas Jackson describes her as being tall, and the scene of Caligula mourning her death in the film *Caligula* (1979), accompanied by Khachaturian's gorgeous music, is unforgettable. Euripides seemed to think the gods envied us the intensity of our mortality, and here Drusilla seeks to remind them of it.

Larry Johnson was born in Natchez, MS, and grew up in Jackson. He attended Mississippi College (BA) and the University of Arkansas (MA, MFA). The author of two books of poetry (*Veins*, David Robert Books, 2009, and *Alloy*, David Robert Books, 2014), he has taught at Alma College, the University of New Orleans, North Carolina State University, Louisburg College, and Wake Tech Community College. In the fall of 2006, he gave a reading of his poetry at the Library of Congress. He lives in Pomona, CA.

Two Poems

GEORGE KALOGERIS

The Handbook of Epictetus

Meletai Thanatos: Meditate on Death.
Acknowledge his silent, implacable approach.
Then steady your heart by focusing your dread.

Practice this lesson each day and you'll be ready,
As ready as anybody can be, for Death.
Meletai Thanatos. It's in The Handbook,

Whose Stoic maxims Marcus Aurelius read
As medicine for pain – the pain of living
Made plain as the day is long. In Greek that's neither

Erudite nor oracular, but more
Like sound parental advice. Easy to follow
But hard to live up to. *Meletai Thanatos*.

"I meditate daily on Death, and how the empire
Will come to an end," the Roman emperor said.
Marcus Aurelius, Philosopher-Caesar.

What little we know about the great Epictetus
Is that he was born a slave, and walked with a limp.
And set up a school that was free and open to all.

But if it's true that late in his life a woman
Lived with him, and he adopted her child,
Then maybe *Meletai Thanatos* wasn't enough,

Even for him. This too is in The Handbook.

For years I've been teaching Epictetus's *Handbook* (*The Enchiridion*), in translation, to undergraduate students. The students admire the clarity and concision of Epictetus, they "get it," but often find his Stoic maxims to be (and rightfully so, I think) daunting. But what never fails to fascinate them, and warm their feelings toward his tough-minded perspective, is learning that the great philosopher had started out as a slave, and later became a crucial sustaining voice for the Roman Emperor Marcus Aurelius. But now that I am nearing my seventies, I'm finding more and more that underneath the stringencies of the Stoicism, and via the careful and caring, almost parental, repetitions, is a deeply empathetic and tempered understanding of just how difficult life can be. Whether or not the philosopher's late-in-life need for offspring is true, now that I'm feeling my age, and childless, the detail struck home and engendered this poem.

Scylla and Charybdis

He stepped off the curb, and then he jumped back.
He looked both ways: no cars in sight.

He stepped off the curb, and then jumped back,
And down a one-way street he looked

Both ways – that tall young man who looked
As though in the throes of a panic attack.

We were on Main Street, awaiting a bus.
He was on a side street, clutching

A plastic bag from CVS
As tightly as whatever demon

Held him in the grip of its talons.
I wanted to shout: "It's okay, my friend!

You're free to cross. There's nobody coming."
But calling out across the way

Might frighten or embarrass him –
Him caught between what, a rock and a hard place?

Or was it the howling, foaming, dog-headed
Octopus and the whorling Vortex?

The black tarmac unfurled at his feet.
The bright red sign on the pole said STOP.

At the corner of Main and Beal, from the edge
Of the curb, he was looking down, way down,

Both ways . . .

This poem records an event I saw unfold at the bus stop near the bottom of my street. I used tetrameter couplets, both end-stopped and run over, to try and convey the jittery hesitations and frozen panic of the troubled young man unable to cross the street. The cliché, "caught between a rock and a hard place," brought to mind the great scene in the *Odyssey* when Odysseus must pass between the devouring straits of Scylla and Charybdis. The traumatized young man was clutching a CVS bag that for all I knew was filled with the psychotropic meds he needed to ward off the demons inside his head. Something terrifying gaped open before him at the curb, causing him to jump backward in alarm. The myth was suddenly fresh to me – for all the good it did that poor soul, at the intersection.

George Kalogeris's most recent book of poems is *Winthropos* (Louisiana State University, 2021). He is also the author of *Guide to Greece* (LSU), a book of paired poems in translation, *Dialogos*, and poems based on the notebooks of Albert Camus, *Camus: Carnets*. His poems and translations have been anthologized in *Joining Music with Reason*, chosen by Christopher Ricks (Waywiser, 2010). He is the winner of the James Dickey Poetry Prize, the Stephen J. Meringoff Award, and the Sheila Margaret Motton Prize.

DAVID M. KATZ

After the Fall

Nothing could be more beautiful than the real.
Watch Icarus walking wingless on the ground,
At his ease, no story any longer to uphold
But that of this day. The young man,
Now fully free of any father's bidding,
Strides easily in the webless air.
He is no longer made, no longer of high
Aspirations. What he was to become
Is now complete, and at a safe distance from the sun.
The air is cool and bright and the road
Beneath his feet and ahead of him.
It is a delight to be unable to fly.

"After the Fall" imagines the myth of Icarus and Daedalus after the familiar tale has ended. To be sure, the notion of Icarus strolling away unscathed after his plunge from the heavens is not (so far as we know) in classical literature. In a poem that elaborates on myth rather than history, however, a contemporary poet may have license to render a new conclusion.

In 2007, in response to a prompt from their teacher, a blogger who administered "Thoughts From 6th Grade," fifteen students devised alternative endings to the myth.[1] One particularly imaginative conclusion, for example, has Icarus discovering "in a potion book that if you mixed butterfly wings, crushed birds beaks, lady bug juice and spider legs together you could make a potion that would make you immortal for 2 hours." Icarus and Daedalus proceed to gulp down the potion, jump through the window of the castle in which they are entrapped, and "hit the ground 500 feet below without a single scratch or bruise." That could well have been the prelude to "After the Fall."

NOTE

[1] See https://tinyurl.com/yr8xya4y (accessed 7/18/24).

David M. Katz is the author of five books of poetry: *The Biographer*, *In Praise of Manhattan*, *Stanzas on Oz*, and *Claims of Home*, all published by Dos Madres Press, and *The Warrior in the Forest*, published by House of Keys Press. Poems of his have appeared in *Poetry*, *The Paris Review*, *The Hudson Review*, *The New Criterion*, *PN Review* (UK), and elsewhere. He posts frequently on his website, *The David M. Katz Poetry Blog* (davidmkatzpoet.com).

Poems and an Essay

KARL KIRCHWEY

Philoctetes

The cave had two mouths.
One spoke outrage, the other self-pity
to anyone who would listen.

At both of them after dark
were the bloody retinal reflections
of wild beasts, even when I felt calm.

I remember a constant thirst.
I broke the ice on the standing pool
to view myself in the shards.

In the sand I wrote WHERE IS IT WRITTEN
THAT VIRTUE WILL ALWAYS ATTEND YOU
big enough to be seen from the air.

My enemies' motions, when they came,
were always unexpected,
though I thought about nothing else.

Then one day I found a bone on the beach
left over from an earlier sacrifice,
and the upward sweep of its lamina,

the tiny holes for nerves drilled through,
even the gape of its foramen,
seemed eloquent with a lost purpose.

When I woke in the morning it had vanished,
my anger, after so many years,
like the telltale and pointer on masts

in a harbor that remained empty.

"When Philoctetes in the Lemnian Isle"

I.

For forty years, the literature and civilization of ancient Greece and Rome have been a recurring presence in my poetry. To my regret, I never learned either ancient Greek or Latin. Instead, this influence seems to have been the result of a geographical accident.

In the early 1970s, I was living with my family in Lausanne, Switzerland. My father hit upon the idea of summer vacations on a Greek island, but instead of Mykonos or Santorini, he took us to the island of Lemnos in the northern Aegean. I was fourteen years old when this began, and I had no idea of how mythologically important this location was: not only the place where the forge god Hephaestus fell to earth, after being thrown out of heaven, but also the site of the ten-year exile of the wounded Greek archer Philoctetes, before his heroic return to the Trojan War. Somehow, those three summer vacations provided me access, not only to a parched and beautiful August landscape, but also to a world of events that have constituted a sort of moral and historical substrate for me, in understanding my own life and the era in which I live.

For many years, I taught a college course called "Classical Myth and the Contemporary Imagination" that juxtaposed Athenian tragedies read in translation with modern and contemporary poets' updates of them: Sophocles's *Oedipus the King* with Rita Dove's *The Darker Face of the Earth*, Euripides's *Alcestis* with T.S. Eliot's *The Cocktail Party*, and so forth. Students (usually not Classics majors) were invited to consider the ancient plays, but also to contemplate the changes in those plays made by modern poets, and the reasons for these changes. While my qualifications for teaching this course do not include being a scholar of the ancient Mediterranean world, as a poet I have been fascinated by the idea of contemporary poets writing for the dramatic stage. This fascination even led me to write my own update of Euripides's *Alcestis*.

In the fall of 2023, I taught the course again for the first time in ten years. In my class I had several Classics majors, but I also had two students from the Business School, one from the College of Health and Human Services, one studying Ecology and Conservation Biology, two pre-meds, and one Computer Science major. In organizing the syllabus, I could have had no way of knowing that our discussion of Sophocles's *Philoctetes* and Irish poet Seamus Heaney's 1990 version called *The Cure at Troy* would more or less coincide with the October 7, 2023 Hamas attack on Israel and with Israel's military retaliation in Gaza.

Sophocles's play concerns Philoctetes's unappeasable rage at his fellow Greeks, including Odysseus, who abandoned him on the desert island of Lemnos for ten years because of an incurable wound caused by a snakebite on his foot. It falls to Odysseus to figure out how to bring Philoctetes back on board; he does this initially by means of a shill, Achilles's son Neoptolemus, who in his mature identity as Pyrrhus horrifyingly slaughters King Priam of Troy at the altar in Vergil's *Aeneid*, but who in Sophocles's account is an untested and idealistic young man. Sophocles is able to resolve this plot only by means of a *deus ex machina* involving the demigod Heracles. Heaney's text is largely a faithful translation of Sophocles's original, which, by means of occasional Irish dialect and above all by a series of rhymed interpolations for the Chorus, manages to provide a parable of the need for forgiveness in the midst of the Troubles in Ireland. Heaney's play premiered at the Field Day Theatre Company in Derry in 1990, eight years before the Easter Accords that brought a halt to decades of sectarian conflict. Just as it is said that both Germans and French in the audience applauded at a performance of Jean Anouilh's *Antigone* in the occupied city of Paris in January of 1944, so apparently Heaney's play drew both the Prime Minister of Northern Ireland and Gerry Adams from Sinn Fein, the political wing of the Irish Republican Army.

Our classroom discussion of the two plays therefore took place at a charged historical moment. The students themselves chose not to raise directly the possible parallels between what happened so long ago on the island of Lemnos or what happened not so long ago in Ireland and what might be driving the Hamas attacks or the Israeli response, but such parallels lent urgency to their consideration of the grudges someone can bear for years after being wronged, the desire for revenge, and the final need for forgiveness and the realization that we share many feelings and reactions with our bitterest enemies. "You must love your crooked neighbor / With your crooked heart," reads part of Heaney's epigraph to *The Cure at Troy*, a quotation from W. H. Auden's poem "As I Walked Out One Evening."

During one of those visits to Lemnos long ago, I had picked up a bone while I was walking on the beach. It was a vertebra, scoured by the sand and the sea, bleached white and shaped like an abstract sculpture. I imagined that it was left over from some sacrifice to the gods by Odysseus's men before they left for Troy, either the first time or the second. From an ox? A sheep? I brought the bone to class, and it passed from hand to hand among the students. One student wondered whether maybe it came from a dolphin. I told my students that this bone had magic powers; that touching it would bring them good fortune. It did not have the complicated identity of Philoctetes's magic bow, symbolic of both friendship and murder.

II.

I have never felt able to write a poem of my own linking Sophocles's parable of forgiveness – or Heaney's – with a particular geopolitical conflict. However, the poetry of place has been central to my own work. The landscape of Lemnos was marked for me partly by the fact that my mother died suddenly between the second and third summers of our visits. In the late fall of 2006, the sweet smell of decaying figs on a tree in our backyard in the Philadelphia suburbs led me to the following sonnet:

ΛΗΜΝΟΣ
"the deep male growl of the sea-lashed headland"
– Philoctetes

August long ago, the summer Lemnian
(not like the deeds of those who killed their men),
the self a glowing bead, like Hephaestus falling
daylong out of heaven in the old story,
the island's interior a forge, a glory-hole,
the odor of wild thyme borne offshore steadily,
the Aegean Sea purple, wine-dark, without epithet;
and as I walked on the beach, my mother not long dead,
the perfect crystal of my self-regard
so lately flawed, and landscape made to echo
my own low cry in the island's empty places,
I found a pure white bone that wind and salt
had scoured of every grief and all self-pity:
and so I came to the love of others.

The initial appearance of that desert island, then, was as a theater for my own first awakening out of childhood's narcissism and, through my mother's death, into an awareness of the lives of others: a variation, I suppose, on the theme of Sophocles's play.

Although Wordsworth never visited Lemnos, in 1827 he, too, wrote a sonnet about Lemnos:

> When Philoctetes in the Lemnian isle
> Like a Form sculptured on a monument
> Lay couched; on him or his dread bow unbent
> Some wild Bird oft might settle and beguile

> The rigid features of a transient smile,
> Disperse the tear, or to the sigh give vent,
> Slackening the pains of ruthless banishment
> From his loved home, and from heroic toil.
> And trust that spiritual Creatures round us move,
> Griefs to allay which Reason cannot heal;
> Yea, veriest reptiles have sufficed to prove
> To fettered wretchedness, that no Bastille
> Is deep enough to exclude the light of love,
> Though man for brother man has ceased to feel.

What is characteristic and beautiful here is that the wounded hero's relationship with nature while on the island – he is either predator or (without his bow) prey – is infused with a Romantic sensibility, so that "spiritual creatures" provide him with a comfort and a love that is not available to human reason. This combats the ruthlessness of his fellow-soldiers' decision to abandon him years earlier and the cruelty of his imprisonment in an open-air Bastille different from the one Wordsworth knew in the days of 1789.

III.

In returning to *Philoctetes* now, I have discovered that I am looking at the play differently from the way I did ten years ago. Of course, this is always the case with certain powerful literary texts. We learn something different each time we return to them. What had happened to me during the interval was really very minor, compared with being marooned for ten years on a desert island: nothing more than a professional disappointment. I had been recruited as an agent of change for an academic program populated by a longtime faculty that had no intention of abiding any change. The usual academic politics ensued. The acrimony of those I had assumed I would be able to greet as colleagues left me initially baffled and finally enraged, and though I resigned as director of the program a year and a half after my arrival, there followed years of brooding over the injustice, as I saw it, of what I had experienced. I had blundered – that is what someone I had counted as a friend told me I had done – into a sacred precinct and was bitten on the foot, I thought, through no fault of my own. The feeling of injustice at this, and at my abandonment by those who had hired me, was deepened by the fact that I had served previously and successfully in a variety of roles both inside and outside of academia. Philoctetes, a hero before his wounding and an exile afterwards, suffered from a deep humiliation, and so did I.

I am tempted to say that only the passage of time and circumstances can heal certain emotional injuries. I look back now on my own bitterness and discover that for the most part I no longer feel it. In a moment of revelation in Sophocles's play, Philoctetes admits to Neoptolemus that his fear of a future with more wrong in it is even stronger than his grievances about the past. In my own case, I did not suffer from Philoctetes's literal isolation – except that certain kinds of self-pity can be profoundly isolating. Eventually I served in a different administrative capacity at the university I had joined, helping me both to change my focus and to feel that I was making a useful contribution to the community. The thing I cared so much about – the future of a particular program – became almost a matter of indifference to me. Like Philoctetes, I have aged; unlike him, the weird volcanic heat of my anger seems to have cooled. On this most recent trip to the desert island of Lemnos, I recognized something in Philoctetes as an aspect of myself.

January 2024

Karl Kirchwey's eighth book of poems, *Good Apothecary*, is forthcoming from Northwestern University Press. He has edited the anthologies *Poems of Rome* and *Poems of Healing* for the Everyman's Library Pocket Poets Series. He is currently working on translations for a first *Selected Poems* in English by Italian poet Giovanni Giudici (1924-

2011), and on a memoir about World War II, family, and memory. He is Professor of English and Creative Writing at Boston University, where he teaches in the MFA Program in Creative Writing. He also teaches for the Classics Department and in the MFA Program in Literary Translation.

RACHEL A. LOTT

Caesar and the Rose

Caesar and the rose are dead.
Senseless we laid them in the earth.
Two living souls they were by birth;
in death how little dust instead.

In death a riddle. For with art
we say a rose un-roses there,
for neither here nor anywhere
was rose without a beating heart.

Is there a rose we speak of now?
There *was* a rose but now is not.
Names may not mean the things we thought,
but if they lose their sense, then how –

– how shall we speak? Each Caesar knows
that death may steal a sense away
and leave its dust. But still today
we speak of Caesar and the rose.

We stir the dust of things once said
as if they lived or yet may be,
and from the ground they rise undead.
The sense they speak is poetry.

 Caesar was a problem for medieval philosophy, mostly because he died. The philosophers wondered how we can talk about things that no longer exist. Roses posed a similar problem, since they became extinct in winter (or so the medievals thought), and the same problem attended anything else deceased. "Caesar" might thus stand for the entire ancient world, indistinguishable in his non-existence from anything else that had perished. Unlike Caesar, the roses would bloom again; but like Caesar, any dead thing was an un-thing during its period of extinction.
 So what could "Caesar" possibly mean? The problem was analogous to a glitch in modern computer programming. If a snippet of code includes a constant and then the constant is deleted, the program returns an error message and possibly breaks. Why wouldn't natural language do the same?

This conundrum turned up during my doctoral research on medieval philosophy of language. The ancient grammarians and logicians, especially Anicius Manlius Severinus Boethius, had argued that names signified both real things and ideas. "Signification" included what we would now call both sense and reference. The medievals accepted this view from antiquity, noted that it created problems for dead things, and tried to find solutions. One medieval theory was that names for dead things became equivocal. Like "bank" and "bank" in English, the name "Caesar" had multiple senses and/or references. "Caesar" could signify the man before his death and a non-being afterwards, or a concept of either of the two.

I was intrigued by this solution, as well as by another idea I'd found in medieval writing: equivocal language was the stuff of poetry. While I was writing my dissertation, I tried to grasp in poetry what I was grappling with in philosophy. We speak of the dead all the time and hardly notice how strange it is. But it is strange. The medievals were the first to notice this uncanniness of our speech, and a full explanation eluded them as much as the ancient logicians and modern programmers. Equivocally speaking, poetry can raise the dead. Perhaps it is this power that makes poetry useful for keeping the study of the past alive, whether of the medieval world or of the rose beds of antiquity.

Rachel A. Lott holds a Ph.D. in medieval studies from the University of Toronto, where her dissertation was on philosophy of language. By day she teaches Latin, logic, and algebra to middle school and high school students. By night she writes and translates poetry. Her current passion project is a translation of Angelus Silesius's epigrams. The first volume has appeared as *The Sorcerers' Stone: Alchemical Poems by Angelus Silesius*.

Poems and an Essay

CHARLES MARTIN

On the Gift of the Cyclops

And having been provided with strong drink
(A *premier cru* to complement the crew)
He pointed toward Odysseus with a wink
And said, "I have a secret gift for you."

"What can it be? I haven't got a clue,"
His guest responded. Leaving his repast,
The Cyclops beamed: "Not now – morning will do –
I want this evening's suspense to last!"

But evening ends with predator outclassed
By merely human ingenuity
And left to stew in his own bile and gore.

Those who put in their years before the mast
Dreamt of a landfall they would never see,
The gift their leader had to settle for.

On the Afterlife
    domus exilis Plutonia

I.
Horace believed that when you die, you'll find
Mere emptiness, but it is hard to think
Of everything you value left behind –
Life, liberty, love, food and drink –
And having your expansive vistas shrink
To the "narrow house of nothing" as MacNeice
So coolly rendered it: a pinpoint – blink
Once, and the whole fine shooting match will cease.

Which may explain why he rewrote the lease
In order to attract tenants for whom
Desires would persever or increase –
Not emptiness, but quite another doom:
Here's Sisyphus, now ready to resume
The uphill struggle with his senseless stone,
And Ariadne tending to her loom,
Doing forever what gets never done.

II
Among the varied afterlives proposed,
A dreamless slumber may be held the best:
All debts paid off in full, the ledger closed.
And yet the notion that we're repossessed,
Brought back again against our will, impressed
In someone's sit-com, somehow satisfies
A need we have not wholly to divest
Ourselves of living when our body dies.

What does it take for us to exorcise
Those presences we still seem to regret?
Are they shed at once? After many tries?
Or is it just possible we've been preset
To carry on all through eternity
With the little tics and tricks of OCD?

III

Then what of that recurrent dream wherein
I am upbraided for my negligence
By our family pet, the poodle Gwen,
Who, though long dead, now dreads incontinence?
"It's true," I said: "I thought we could dispense
With daily walks, once – well, once you were gone.
Nor has there turned up any evidence
Of any . . . indiscretions."
                                      "There were none:

Even as you," she said, "I have my own
Obligations, the incessant weight
Of ever-widening responsibility
Gnawing at me as I once gnawed a bone,
And which my death would not eliminate."
"Would mine?" I asked. But she made no reply.

OF PREY AND PREDATORS:
"On the Gift of the Cyclops" and Book 9 of *The Odyssey*

In *Blood Rites*, Barbara Ehrenreich's 1997 investigation into the "origins and history of the passions of war," she argues for the evolutionary continuity of hominid and human experience, beginning in that dim past when our ancestors first entered the grassy arena filled with advanced predators for whom our kind were nothing more than the occasional snack. From that time, when we had no strategy besides avoidance to survive their attentions, we learned to compete with them over countless generations, through negotiation, which led to idealizing and worshipping their power, and through defiance, which led to the development of the mental and physical tools that allowed us to overcome them. Ehrenreich argues that this journey has left its indelible marks on our customs and institutions, even as the memory of it has been suppressed: "The transformation from prey to predator, in which the weak rise up against the strong, is the central 'story' in the early human narrative . . ."

In Book 9 of Homer's *Odyssey*, the first glimpse we have of our eponymous hero in action shows him as a skilled predator – of other humans. Encountering the Kikonians, "I sacked their city and killed their people, / and out of their city taking their wives and many possessions / we shared them out, so none might go cheated of his proper / portion." The Kikonians are unhappy about being treated as a hunter's prey and strike back. It is a near thing, and Odysseus must withdraw, after losing some of his men. After a brief episode among the Lotus Eaters, Odysseus comes to the land of the Cyclopes, whose lives are arranged in a more instinctual way: your typical Cyclops would appear to be a solitary cave dweller, a shepherd, devoid of manners, customs, and institutions, whose writ extends only to his family, if he happens to have one. At the same time, he is semi-divine, the son of Poseidon. For Ehrenreich, Poseidon is only one of the human idealizations of the flesh-eating carnivores who made the lives of our hominid ancestors so brief and worrisome. His cyclopean son Polyphemos is ready to play his role in "the central 'story' in the early human narrative."

Outweighed by Polyphemos and puny in comparison, Odysseus must rely on human wit to devise a plan to overcome the giant and then to employ the physical tools of human cultivation (intoxicating wine and the fire-sharpened stick) to carry it out. What Homer leaves unspoken, of course, is the human sociability and cooperation that allows Odysseus both to devise the plan and to make it succeed. The helpless, niddering hominids who watched the great four-footed predators stalking their prey were perhaps the first to realize how it is done: the hunter must deny his own presence, pretend not to be there, obliterate his own identity so that no one is doing the stalking, no one is lifting the spear – until no one is suddenly a presence and an absence at the same time: "Nobody is killing me by force or treachery."

The story belongs to the conqueror, but Homer does allow us a brief look at these events from the other side. When Odysseus has revealed his true identity to the Cyclops, the latter reveals that he had been told that he would lose the sight of his eye at the hands of Odysseus: "but always I was on the lookout for a man handsome / and tall, with great endowment of strength on him, to come here; / but now the end of it is that a little man, niddering, feeble, / has taken away the sight of my eye, first making me helpless." The prey that has become predator passes such stories of transformation and victory down from generation to generation.

Ezra Pound famously described an epic as "a long poem containing history," but our epics and epic-like poems and works of prose, both ancient and modern, often seem to be more concerned with various aspects of the relationship between predator and prey – who gets to be which, and when? The *Iliad* opens with the rage of Achilles but goes on almost at once to its consequences: that rage resulted in carrion, the warriors whose bodies became "the delicate feasting / of all birds, of dogs, and the will of Zeus was accomplished." When Krishna in the *Bhagavad Gita* reveals his divine form, he shows himself as a carnivorous deity, devouring whole worlds full of helpless men. In Christian epics, that aspect of the divine is taken on by Satan or one of his minions: it is the former who personally masticates the worst of all sinners in the icy pit of the *Inferno*, and in the anonymous *Beowulf*, it is Satan's minion Grendel who preys on the apparently helpless warriors of Hrothgar. The conclusion of our national epic *Moby Dick* provides us with a reversal of the story of human triumph that Homer tells in the *Odyssey*, as prey turns into predator, and an even later epic-like poem, *The Wasteland* has a section called "The Burial of the Dead," in which T.S. Eliot deals with the problems entailed in making sure the dead don't come back again:

> There I saw one I knew, and stopped him, crying: "Stetson!
> "You who were with me in the ships at Mylae!
> "That corpse you planted last year in your garden,
> "Has it begun to sprout? Will it bloom this year?
> "Or has the sudden frost disturbed its bed?
> "Oh keep the Dog far hence, that's friend to men,
> "Or with his nails he'll dig it up again!

The questions he raises and the warnings he issues seem to have followed us from far away and long ago: the one who digs it up again may come for us. The contest has not ended: it is brought back to mind whenever we read of a hiker fatally surprised in the woods by a mountain lion or a grizzly bear, or of a great saurian swiftly emerging from an algae-covered canal on the edge of a golf course in search of a fast meal at the eighteenth hole.

[Note: All quotations from either the *Odyssey* or the *Iliad* are from Richmond Lattimore's translations of these poems.]

Charles Martin's eighth book of poems, *The Khayyam Suite*, will be published by the Johns Hopkins University Press in the spring of 2025. A former Poet in Residence at the Cathedral of St. John the Divine in New York City, his version of Euripides's *Medea* was published in 2019 by the University of California Press, and his translation of Ovid's *Metamorphoses* has just been reprinted in the Norton Library series.

ZACHARY McGAR

The Chorus

We have again been called to witness
As tragedy becomes commonplace.
We are accustomed to the worst outcomes:
Each morning we don our gowns and masks
To make the long commute to the palace
And watch our hopes curl up and burn
Like the smoking stub of Phaethon.

We have waited for our turn to speak.
We've been polite, we've deferred
And danced around their discomfort.
Then they say that we complain too much,
But we know we're only talking to ourselves.
How typical of our dynamic: they brought us up
On stage only to belittle and ignore us.

They have criminalized their discomfort:
It's against the law to inconvenience them,
An offense to serve them without a smile.
They'll be damned if they let anyone
Inconvenience them; but let them offer up
Some half-mast flags and half-assed prayers.
And though our masks look shocked, we aren't.

They have the audacity to insult our outrage,
Mock our consciences, condemn our convictions
As weaknesses rather than the kernels of courage!
Oh it is such an honor to be moved to tears so often,
But the tears that wet our eyes must sharpen our perception.
We are under no obligation to go easy on them.
They don't get to call down gods they don't obey.

We shall wrench the world from under their feet.
We shall outlive them, their laws, and their rites,
And be witnesses to their final hours, when at last

The Furies crack their hearts open like pomegranates.
It will be an honor to witness the world changing.
That is what we shall call catharsis, when at last
They are left to mop our stage clean with their tears.

This poem began as a short prose piece in which a chorus member in a production of Aeschylus's *Agamemnon* suddenly loses his grip on reality and believes he needs to set things right and rescue Agamemnon from a fatal bath. Although that story has never seen more than three pairs of eyes, the idea at its center – *what if the chorus rebelled?* – stuck with me and insisted upon its own star vehicle. With every drama that I read through college and graduate school, the idea would ask, "Could the chorus just *talk* to Theseus about this?"; or, "Would it really be so bad if one of them slapped Creon across the face?"

Although the idea remained an amusing game to comfort me in the face of An Awful Lot of Reading throughout school, it took on a darker significance in a time of proud, even gleeful regression in American culture. In *Agamemnon* the chorus members lament their doddering ineffectuality as feeble old men not involved in the great enterprise of the Trojan War. Bearing witness to these past few relentless years has made me feel much the same way, as though I were standing outside the palace begging my leaders to resist doing the worst possible thing just this once.

Looking at the chorus as a band of ineffectual sufferers, however, is not an accurate or particularly useful take. The chorus is always there, and always speaking up. Recognition of that finally brought that little thought – *what if the chorus rebelled?* – to fruition in this poem. The chorus has allowed me to speak honestly, to declare a resistance that I have found difficult to articulate for a long time. It has strengthened my resolve to take a place on the stage. Since I first began reading Latin in high school, the Classics have moved me, and I am proud to find in them my own language.

Zachary McGar is a reference librarian in Baton Rouge, LA. He studied Classics at Loyola University New Orleans and the University of Georgia, where he received his MA. His prose and poetry have appeared in *The Stoneslide Corrective* and *Eternal Haunted Summer*. An avid gamer, he has recently become obsessed with translating Lucian's *True Story* into a tabletop adventure.

SUSAN McLEAN

Achilles and Odysseus

Of course they hate each other. One, a sword;
the other, more a river than a rock.
Achilles, when Odysseus brings word
of what the king will give him to come back,
replies, "I hate like Hell's gates one who says
one thing and hides another in his heart."
As much as calls him liar – which he is –
although he stuck to facts in his report.
He mentioned no apology; there's none.
Achilles isn't wrong. Odysseus lies

to everyone: his father, wife, and son;
his men, his slaves, Athena in disguise.
Whatever gets him the desired result.
To him, Achilles is a pride-mad brat,
sharp as a blade, but wobbly in the hilt
and dangerous. Wrapped up in his conceit,
Achilles never takes advice except
from gods, whereas Odysseus pays heed
to everyone – slaves, herdsmen, girls in the street –
and follows their advice if it seems good.

Odysseus, on the shore of death's domain,
is hailed there by Achilles' prickly shade,
and tries to soothe and flatter him again,
praising his high esteem among the dead.
"Don't sweet-talk *me* about death," Achilles snaps.
"Better to be a poor man's half-starved farm hand
than king of the played-out dead." He turns his hopes
to hearing news about his distant homeland,
imagining men mistreating his old father,
asking about the son he never knew –
concerns Odysseus shares. How much he'd rather
be alive! He doesn't say "like you."

When I was an undergraduate reading the *Iliad* and the *Odyssey* for the first time, I read Erich Auerbach's essay "Odysseus' Scar," which argues that Homer's accounts are all surface, no subtext, and that the heroes of Homer's works change little, inside or out. But over the course of thirty years of teaching both epics and re-reading them many times, I concluded that Homer implies many things about his characters that he never states directly, and that some of his main characters change in significant ways as a result of their experiences. In particular, I was struck by the tensions between Odysseus and Achilles on the few occasions that they talk to one another, but particularly in Book 9 of the *Iliad*, when Odysseus is sent to persuade Achilles to return to battle, and in Book 11 of the *Odyssey*, when Odysseus meets the shade of Achilles on the shore of the Underworld. The hostility of the speeches of Achilles to Odysseus on both occasions seems out of line with any provocation from Odysseus, leading me to suspect long-standing resentments on both sides. That gave me the poem's first line: "Of course they hate each other."

But my first attempt to compare the two characters quickly failed. I considered writing in blank verse, but I prefer to write in rhyme, because rhyme is the flashlight I usually use to find my way through the dark of what comes next. In this case, I could not find true rhymes that fit the things I felt I needed to say about the two characters. It was only when I was ready to give up that it occurred to me to use slant rhymes instead. Then, the paired words that spoke to each other started leading me again. Only after I finished the poem did I realize that Achilles and Odysseus themselves are like slant rhymes. At first, one notices mainly the differences between them, and only at the end does it appear that they also have things in common.

I did not study Ancient Greek, so I have depended on translations of Homer, and the speeches of Achilles in my poem are indebted to the wording of the translations by Robert Fagles and Robert Fitzgerald that I used when I was teaching. I am also indebted to Auden for his insight that "poetry might be defined as the clear expression of mixed feelings." To me, the realization of Achilles, too late, that the choices of Odysseus were more successful is made even more poignant by his unwillingness to admit that to Odysseus himself.

Susan McLean's poems and translations have appeared in *The Classical Outlook* many times. She is a retired English professor from Southwest Minnesota State University in Marshall, MN. She has published two books of original poems, *The Best Disguise* and *The Whetstone Misses the Knife*. In 2014, the University of Wisconsin Press published a book of her translations of Martial, *Selected Epigrams*.

GEOFFREY MOVIUS

Meditatio

omnes eodem cogimur, omnium
versatur urna serius ocius
sors exitura et nos in aeternum
exsilium impositura cumbae.
— Horace, *Odes* 2.3

I read yesterday, "The questions one never thought to ask
the dead pile up." As do those dead – friends, family, others.
You just can't tell when that visit or distant wave, nod, shout
might be a last sighting. Tiring to be so much on the alert,
thinking your final appearance will be the one remembered.

That matter of questions unasked is daunting, too. Suddenly
you might never know an answer. And soon as impossibility
sets in, answers become unimportant, forgotten, consigned
to the bin with all the rest. Heavens! What an unnerving outcome:
where once there was a known resource, there is now nothing
saying nothing. One person knew and that person's gone.

What of all I'll take down with me? What am I alone privy to?
Who will wonder what I knew so well? What will be lost?
Someone somewhere who loved me or was loved? I have no
high expectations. Long life brings much to our table to share –
there's no way though to pass it round. I am becoming air
even as I – sooner or later – leave this poem.

When I was a graduate student about sixty years ago, I took a summer school refresher course in Latin. I'd not read Horace in high school but had a brief encounter that summer that stuck fast somewhere in my mind. After ten years of teaching, I changed direction and spent thirty more raising funds for Harvard University. I continued to write poetry – a habit from school years on. Retirement gave me more time for it. I guess in my eighties, that ghost memory was waiting for me. "Meditatio" is in part the result. An old friend and quondam Tufts colleague, John Fyler, helped me track down one plausible classical origin for at least the tenor of my poem: Horace's *Odes* 2.3. The idea that "*serius ocius*" – sooner or later – death comes to everyone, is closer to the front of my mind now than it was in graduate school.

Geoffrey Movius lives in Cambridge, MA. His poetry has appeared in many little magazines, including *Agenda, Boston Review, Chicago Review, Harvard Review, Hesperides, Little Balkans Review, The Little Magazine, London Magazine, Mudfish,* and *Ploughshares. TRANSIT: Selected Poems, 1960-2010* was published in 2012 by Pressed Wafer in Boston. He is working now on another collection.

JULIA NEMIROVSKAYA (AUTHOR) AND BORIS DRALYUK (TRANSLATOR)

Herakles

The centaur's blood burns, eats away my flesh.
I lived in silence, stoppering within me
what I might pour out in a lover's discourse –
but first, one labor, followed by another . . .
I can remember twelve of these at least.
I had been waiting for a chance to open
before a lover, or a son, a friend,
but now I writhe, encased in hot pain's armor,
and no one in the world will ever hear
what I held hidden, a whole lifetime's thoughts.

Mother hesitated over whether to read the last chapter of *The Labors of Herakles* to me, but I insisted. The image of my beloved hero wrapped in a poisoned cloak, with friends standing helplessly around, presented itself to my mind whenever I burnt my finger or had a sore. With his labors behind him, would he share his story with family and friends, perhaps on a wintry night, by the fire? And would my charismatic father, a World War II veteran, physicist, and downhill skier, have shared his hidden story with us if he hadn't died tragically in his fifties? It was always the immediate issues that we discussed – dinner plans or driving directions. With several children, food shortages, emigration, and full-time jobs, my family discussions in the US have also revolved around immediate concerns. Everything I've thought or felt has been collected and hidden in my tiny poems. I never imagined that, as a Russophone poet, I could share them with my Anglophone children or readers in the US. Yet when I met Boris Dralyuk, everything changed. Boris recreates my poems in a new language. It often feels like he has lived my life – from the childhood books of Greek mythology to the attempts to capture experiences in words – and knows how to translate not just poems but my whole life into English.

Julia Nemirovskaya is a Russophone poet and prose writer. Born in Moscow in 1962, she immigrated to the United States in 1990 and teaches Russian literature and culture at the University of Oregon. She has published three collections of poems – *Moia knizhechka* (*My Little Book*, 1998), *Vtoraia knizhechka* (*Second Little Book*,

2014), and *Slyshnee* (*More Audible*, 2021) – as well as the novel *Lis* (2017). English translations of her poems have appeared in *Washington Square Review*, *Exchanges*, *Asymptote*, and other journals.

Boris Dralyuk is the author of *My Hollywood and Other Poems* (Paul Dry Books, 2022) and the translator of Isaac Babel, Andrey Kurkov, Maxim Osipov, and other authors. His poems, translations, and criticism have appeared in the *NYRB*, the *TLS*, *The New Yorker*, *Best American Poetry 2023*, and elsewhere. Formerly editor-in-chief of *The Los Angeles Review of Books*, he is currently a Tulsa Artist Fellow and teaches in the Department of English and Creative Writing at the University of Tulsa.

SUZANNE NOGUERE

At mihi te comitem iuraras usque futuram –
per me perque oculos, sidera nostra, tuos.
Verba puellarum, foliis leviora caducis,
irrita, qua visum est, ventus et unda ferunt.
— Ovid, *Amores* 2.16.43-46

Your Eyes,

our stars we wish upon as clouds disperse
like curtains drawn aside to show the night
spectacular because your twin-star blaze
in splendor sends your essence through the air
to charm us as you morph from youth to man
and make us wish your future be so bright:
"Star light, star bright, first star I see tonight . . ."

But to the girl in bed alone your eyes,
which double for a heavenly body, burn,
draw longing out, and turn her sighs to words
that crystallize her secret as she yearns
again, "I wish I may, I wish I might,
have the wish I wish tonight": yourself;
and, gazing at the wall, imagines there
the zodiac of future loves lit by
your eyes, twin stars that usher summer's heat.

And we who could attest those stars are eyes,
and radiance the gladness they inspire,

are yet the wishers who would promise most,
proclaiming surety of astral glow.
The constellation of all dreams glides west
when you illuminate a path ahead,
parting the darkness with your eyes, our stars.

As a student at Barnard in the 1960s, I took first-year Latin at Columbia because of a scheduling conflict. The textbook for the course was John F. C. Richards's *Essentials of Latin: An Introductory Course Using Selections from Latin Literature*. No text could have been more thrilling! By Lesson XI, the exercises were famous lines of Latin poetry; even as snippets they were glorious. The passage above from Ovid appeared in Lesson XXIV. I loved it but also found its characterization of girls provocative. I wanted to turn it on its head with a love poem from a girl's perspective. I didn't know that translators would render "sidera nostra" as "my stars" rather than "our stars." I took the plural possessive literally and put my poem in the voice of an unnamed group of adults who admire the exceptional young man whom the girl has fallen in love with. When I wrote the poem, I was that girl. Now, fifty-odd years later, I'm among the group of sympathetic elders who frame the poem.

Suzanne Noguere is the author of a poetry collection, *Whirling Round the Sun*, and two children's books. With James V. Hatch she co-wrote a novel and the musical play *Klub Ka: The Blues Legend*, which was performed at La MaMa E.T.C. in New York City, where she lives. With artist Miriam Adams she created the art/poetry series *Leaf Lines*, now in the collection of the Northern New England Museum of Contemporary Art.

EUGENE O'CONNOR

Tiresias in Hell

An Edith Sitwell turban
on his head, his fingers, like hers,
blood-tipped poniards,
he goes, with rocking motions
of his womanly, broad hips
on tiny feet.

From a capacious handbag
he dispenses leaves
of writing full of prophecies,
the kind they put in fortune cookies,
vaguely adaptable
to the occasion.

A ghost of himself, knowing
the paths of past and future,
but nothing of the here and now,
he rants of "What I was" –

a speaker in tongues, a ventriloquist,
female impersonator, a liver
of false lives,

and then his budding interest
in the tarot cards and tea leaves.
"Do you want
your fortune told? I've got it
written down. I wrote it
in the war (I was a German)

at my kitchen table, its
regular checked cloth
an ordered symbol of the cosmos,
of checkerboards and chess.
Here, take and read.
As the Cumaean Sibyl used to prophesy,
shuffling dry leaves like playing cards:
I bring good news."

Like Janus looking forward and back, Tiresias is a liminal figure mediating between male and female, mortals and the gods, blindness and sight, present and future, this world and the afterworld. I saw him as a drag personality, grandiose and affected, who has a sort of nightclub act. There is in fact a drag artist who calls himself Tiresias (a.k.a. Evan Silver), who performs at a cabaret called The Brick in the Williamsburg neighborhood in Brooklyn, NY. He/she, suffering from a degenerative eye disease, explores an inner sight that envisions a queer utopia.

Eugene O'Connor (Columbus, OH) is a classicist and retired book editor, whose articles, poems, and translations have appeared in numerous print and online journals and collections. His books include *Symbolum Salacitatis: A Study of the God Priapus as a Literary Character* and *The Essential Epicurus*. He is co-author, with K. W. Goings, of *The Classics in Black and White: Black Colleges, Classics Education, Resistance, and Assimilation* (University of Georgia Press, 2024).

SAFFRON ORFFAS

On First Reading the Loeb Catullus, Carmen 64

The imagination can be captured by the finest of nets,
slung quietly in the unexpecting shade.
And so perhaps it should not have been so surprising
to find my own entangled by a footnote,* two thin lines,
almost unnoticeable, hanging beneath the wedding song
of Catullus, bright in red boards.

I had read the stanza prior, about the ripples of Scamander,
choked and red with the blood of Ilion, and,
soft and white, about the limbs of Polyxena,
sacrificed for a slain hero in the one that followed.
But look! Here it suggests a stanza lost, connecting them,
a gap which, now seen, I cannot seem to unsee.

Of course. There must once have been another witness,
prophesied to stand between that muddy, bloody river
and that baleful pyre. It would have been a pointer to a battle won,
with gore and anger and sorrow and the clenched fist of victory,
a middle testimony that everything bright and pretty
still contains a darkness, always emerging in the end.

There would've had to have been horses, god-like horses,
clattering on the Trojan plain, glittering arms cast down in the dirt,
and the glory of men turned repulsive in a moment
while gods glanced down, distracted by their music,
and the Fates clucked their tongues and spun their thread;
run ye spindles, drawing out the woof-threads, run.

It must have been allusive, and heroic: we already know
the tale of Achilles' rage and Hector's fault,
so not just the body, but even the splendid epithets
must have been dragged, words pulled along by words,
led across the line by mythical stallions, armor jumbled behind;
run ye spindles, drawing out the woof-threads, run.

We ought to have heard those sisters chattering together that
the thirsty dust of the fields of Dardana will be a witness,
unwilling (for Apollo's sake) to cling to Hector, Shepherd of the Laomedians,
stripped of his shining armor, Xanthus and Balius
dragging his body all about under the whip crack of Achilles,
run ye spindles, drawing out the woof-threads, run.

Instead of tripping over this unkempt seam we should have read that,
testis pulvis Dardaniae sitens erit agri,
haerere ad pastorem Laomedontiadarum,
arma nitentia nudatum, et Xantho Balioque
circumtractum, nolens tum propter Citharoedum;
currite ducentes subtegmina, currite, fusi.

> And, having read it, perhaps we should do more than say
> that once there was a something here, another portion,
> and instead sew on our own patch, matched to the lost hexameters,
> a trembling effort even, wooing the imagination,
> which sometimes, even by the clumsiest of lines,
> can find itself blissfully caught up, and the softest of hints.

*The Loeb Catullus has a footnote following line 361, in between two stanzas in which the Fates call future "witnesses" to the deeds of Achilles, which says: "Lucian Mueller conjectured that a stanza beginning *testis erit* and prophesying the slaying of Hector has been lost after this verse."

The inspiration for this poem came from reading the Loeb edition of Catullus 64, and in particular the footnote to line 361 which says, "Lucian Mueller conjectured that a stanza beginning *testis erit* and prophesying the slaying of Hector has been lost after this verse." When I read that note this past year, almost immediately, like a bird caught in a net, my mind began to imagine what a lost stanza in that spot might have looked like, and my poetic heart to feel real sadness that it had been lost forever.

In the end, all of those feelings turned into a poem, or rather, like Catullus 64, a poem nested within another poem. I don't much believe in the Muses in an ontological sense, but I do think that when your heart whispers something for you to write, you just need to write it. Stanza seven, then, is my own composition (which is translated into English in stanza six), and is the result of imagining and trying to recreate something that didn't otherwise exist, except for its shadow, drawing hints and suggestions from the context, and doing my best to match the style and meter of Catullus. It was written to fit in there and bridge the possible gap after line 361, but also to fit where it does here, as a way of expressing the emotion and the journey of having encountered this other poem of Catullus in such a fresh and unexpected way.

Similar to the way that Carmen 64 skirts along the edge of classical mythological themes which would all have been known to its original audience, my poem as a whole is written along the edge of the main narrative of Catullus, asking the reader to re-engage with a known text in a fresh way. In writing it, I was also influenced by "On First Looking into Chapman's Homer," which John Keats wrote the morning after binge reading the *Iliad* straight through one night with a friend, flushed with the excitement of discovery.

That's how the Loeb Catullus made me feel. I had known Catullus (a bit, at least), and known Carmen 64, but that one note, in this particular version, business-like translation and all, somehow transported me back into the life of the poem, not only as if I was reading it for the first time, but almost like catching a glimpse of the feelings and ideas that rolled through the heart of Catullus when he first wrote it.

Saffron Orffas began studying Latin as a hobby during the lockdown of autumn 2021 through (the excellent) *Gustatio Linguae Latinae* online. With fluency in both Bahasa Indonesia and English, as well as a humanities BA from outside the US, Saffron has lived in the American South since 2021, reading a good bit of Latin, and working to compose verse that captures the best of the later Roman poets, the kind that riles the passion of lovers, goads the noxious, and brings many a smile to the lips of friends old and new.

JAMES OWENS

Love Poem as Abandoned Greek Soldier

> *. . . per sidera testor,*
> *per superos atque hoc caeli spirabile lumen . . .*
> *– Aeneid* 3.599-600

As if sucking stones from sour fruit and gnawing the marly roots of weeds,
Cowering in holes while giants lurched above my hiding places,

As if I were Achaemenides, son of the impoverished Adamastus,
With nothing against Troy, who enlisted from the bite of destitution,

Whom slippery Ulysses deserted in the blood-foul den of the Cyclopes,
Be it carelessly, for lack of friends to guard my back, or as bait,

As meat and a warm frothing of gore to slow pursuit, as if I have scrounged
And starved for months in the spiny thickets and on the rotting cliffs,

As I held to the most ragged, feverish scruff of life, until I envied
The release from grief that certain of my fellows earned in hostile jaws –

But now you are on the shore at dawn, you like the whole fleet of Trojans,
Fulgent with bronze on the bright sand, the Mediterranean glittering

And cerulean behind you, as the ships swell and dip on its profound bosom,
And I stagger ragged and reduced from the still dark-glutted woods, tottering

In your surprised direction, falling to my knees to embrace your knees,
Not imagining myself restored to myself, not yet, not after such labours,

Compelled only to stretch my hands toward mercy, imploring rescue or death:
I swear by the stars, by those presences above, by the heavens' inhalable light.

The third book of the *Aeneid* is great fun, if one does not hurry past it on the way from the fall of Troy to Dido's heartbreak. Though the book can seem a *bricolage* of incidents and episodes, it is here that Aeneas's character is both revealed and forged, as he learns to become the leader of a people in exile, and many of the dilemmas that the Trojans face in Book Three foreshadow events later in the poem. Aeneas's treatment of Achaemenides, a Greek who has gotten himself left behind on the island of the Cyclopes, seems to me a commentary on the hero's final, defining action in Book Twelve, his killing of the helpless Turnus. Here, guided by his father's example, Aeneas shows mercy toward a vulnerable enemy; there, ignoring the very specific instruction he has received from Anchises in Hades, he butchers the overthrown Turnus and sets in motion the blood-soaked cascade of history that will culminate in Rome's civil wars (making "pious Aeneas" the most deplorable failure in all of classical literature).

The decision to turn this historically fraught episode into a love poem from Achaemenides's point of view might not make immediate sense, but perhaps any lover approaches the beloved in much the same spirit as the desolate

Greek soldier who seeks rescue, that is, from a place of vulnerability, in need of generosity and mercy. My irresistible response to those lines was to remember approaching my beloved, at our first meeting, in a similar destitution, pleading for health, and receiving from her a similar grace. Perhaps this treatment of the poem is not a stretch? *Amor* is a particular way of living in *caritas,* as her example teaches me.

James Owens's most recent book is *Family Portrait with Scythe* (Bottom Dog Press, 2020). His translations of Latin poetry have appeared in *Arion, Dappled Things, Wild Court,* and *Ezra: An Online Journal of Translation,* among others. He earned an MFA at the University of Alabama and lives in a small town in northern Ontario, Canada.

BASIL PERKINS

Corinna Comes, Once Again

Iusta precor: quae me nuper praedata puella est,
aut amet aut faciat, cur ego semper amem!
— Ovid, *Amores* 1.5.1-2

. . . nonne satis fuerat timidae inclamasse puellae,
nec nimium rigidas intonuisse minas,
aut tunicam a summa diducere turpiter ora
ad mediam? – mediae zona tulisset opem.
— Ovid, *Amores* 1.7.45-48

corinna comes. beseeches you, her poet. hopes this finds
poet lover well, in a hot room midday with
the sundials beating their noon hour and
the husbands away with affairs unspeakable.

for this poetess's words will be burned, by future-past
fanatic of things moored in this same marble, by men not
such as you, lover: dear ovid poet lover, exiled poor poet.
therefore, you, ovid, find the snag in the fabric. and, you, ovid, weave
the story through it, ovid. your corinna beseeches you. heed her request.

may we know how to weave in the way of penelope. may we, by day,
continue to weave our own funeral shroud so as to please those that would
harm us. let us survive. let us too slip in our new morals unnoticed, and
let that be the reason you have abandoned, for tomis, a corinna, who remains
unable to notice you and your bruised, rosy, dawn-colored lips.

and at night, may the woven binds, they themselves learn how to unwind as
they are seen in a different candlelight, the shroud of words such as these,
such as yours. may the epithets and the riddles and the untouchable
stories of old, be more threads still woven into that knot which
makes itself up for untying. a tunic which makes itself up for ripping
so that we may learn where to cut our own strings. may the stories
cut sharp, razors of their own right.

parody their greed. wring out the woven stories,
damp from sitting out in the rain and retell their precious
mythologies with clever elisions, careful additions, your tongue
and your cheek were ever told to be too pleasing.

let us inch forward in warm hope. let us survive to liveable
times.

This poem is in direct response to Ovid's first book of *Amores*, drawing linguistic inspiration for lines directly from the source text. It is told from the perspective of a reflective and longing Corinna, purported (by Ovid) to be the lover of Ovid. It hopes to spur questions about the ancients' impact on contemporary systems of gender. The poem also speaks to a revolutionary and rebellious Ovid, one whose poetry was not wholly frivolous, but rather whose writings practiced dissent.

Basil Perkins (they/them) is an emerging scholar of ancient gender and imperialism, with a fervent love of classical reception and queer studies. Currently, they are a graduate student at the University of Georgia.

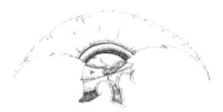

TRISH REEVES

At the Library of the Baths of Trajan

an entire audience draped in wool,
stone steps to lounge on, and who
would you want to stand before you
and the twenty-one niches
filled with leather buckets of scrolls –
half in Latin, half in Greek –
while she read something new, and then
the old favorites? I've tipped my hand
with a pronoun. Yet, if seated there,
I'd have been around seven-hundred years

too late to expect her, even then, even if
she'd been willing to travel by sea
and by cart to remind all who came after
the very fine and martial Homer
that Anaktoria could be wooed
by a woman who knew to speak,
at last, the lyric *I*, and bring her
lover home.

"At the Library of the Baths of Trajan" came about after I was given a book last year, *The Library, A World History* libraries from across the ancient and modern world. Almost every photo caused me to want to enter that particular library.

However, I was most drawn to the library in Trajan's Forum in Rome. This library, the Bibliotheca Ulpia, now exists in ruins, and it is uncertain whether or not it is actually Trajan's library. One of the reasons it is considered so is because the deep niches in the remaining curved wall appear to be the correct size to hold wooden cabinet inserts that would have been there to protect the scrolls. Another reason is that it faces, from the other side of Trajan's Column, a very similar ruin, conforming to a Roman design for libraries: one building for Greek scrolls facing another building for Latin scrolls. In "At the Library of the Baths of Trajan," line six, the scrolls in both languages are found in the same building, likely an inaccurate detail, though indicative of the importance of both languages in ancient Rome.

And all of the above, of course, is to ignore the heart of the poem. It was not only a beautiful book and four years of high school Latin that led me to this scene I set in the Library of Trajan, although they can't be denied. But it was also the "lyric *I*" of Sappho, her stirring poem to Anaktoria, and the longing undoubtedly known to most poets for one more of those few unforgettable readings one was privileged to attend. For me the last Goddard readings always remain: Louise Glück reading an astonishingly large number of poems she'd written in the preceding ten days ("Mock Orange" among them); and the readings on the following nights, Ellen Bryant Voigt, Charles Simic, Stephen Dobyns, Tom Lux. The heart never quiets.

Trish Reeves's fellowships for her poetry include those from the National Endowment for the Arts, Yaddo, and the Kansas Arts Commission. Her poetry has appeared in *Ploughshares*, *The Women's Review of Books*, *New Letters*, *Leon Literary Review*, etc. Her first book, *Returning the Question*, won the Cleveland State University Poetry Center Prize; her most recent book, *The Receipt*, was published in 2023 by Cynren Press. For twenty-one years, Reeves was on the English faculty of Haskell Indian Nations University, and led Changing Lives Through Literature for Johnson County Kansas Corrections. Currently she is a Humanities Kansas Scholar.

DAN ROSENBERG

The Roses of Heliogabalus

after Alma-Tadema

crammed with storm   in the ire-flow of painterly

    kitsch   petals   drifting endless bodies

        rendered   motion   pink as pink

everywhere   another Etna   the pretty   the dead

    redhead staring out   a suffering or source   before

        what is still: metal shadow distance
                                      column-colored arm
                                      feasters looking looking

        the riot of stink   their lungs thick-petalled

marvel   drowning inside   briefly this beauty   snarled

& rent   only to end   gaze-buried

        but where is the refuse pile   the mountainous

stems & thorns   the other revelers   their blood

    let by knowing   alive therein

Ekphrasis means *description*, and for most of the history of ekphrastic poetry, it described art, rendering verbally that which had been rendered visually. The appeal of straightforward description in the pre-modern world is obvious: Without the technology to easily reproduce and distribute an image, a beautiful description is a fine consolation prize. Since the advent of photography, and certainly the internet, the need for that traditional mode of ekphrasis has gone the way of the photorealistic portrait painting.

To write ekphrastically now can mean any mode of engagement with an artwork: to imagine oneself into the perspective of the artist, a figure depicted in the work, a museum patron viewing it, etc. John Hollander differentiates between actual ekphrasis, which responds to existing works of art, and "notional ekphrasis," which takes fictional works of art as its subject. (Notably, the fountainhead of ekphrasis, Homer's description of Achilles's shield in the *Iliad*, is actually notional: the shield as described could not have been crafted by mortal hands.)

My poem is actual ekphrasis, responding to Alma-Tadema's painting, but I have always been drawn to what ekphrasis can *add* in its conversation with art. I tried to capture in the poem some of the dislocatedness I experience when looking at the painting. The impetus for this dislocation is not just the swirling flower petals, but the characters' expressions. The figures in the background, the teenaged Roman emperor Heliogabalus and

The Roses of Heliogabalus (1888), Laurence Alma-Tadema.
(https://tinyurl.com/yc8pju2p). Accessed 7/17/24.

his company, seem amused by what they're watching, suggesting familiar voyeuristic excess, but what about the woman on the bottom-right? Or the bottom-left? Both turn toward the viewer with wide eyes, implicating us in the very voyeurism that the painting seems to condemn. It's an unsettling image that only gets more unsettling as we learn more about its origins: Heliogabalus allegedly caused his banquet guests to be smothered under flowers he had dropped from the ceiling.

My poem aims to share my wondering with the reader, a wondering that bleeds beyond the frame. My favorite moment in any ekphrastic poem is in Keats's "Ode on a Grecian Urn," when he stops describing what's on the urn and instead imagines the empty town whose inhabitants are captured on the urn's surface. That expansion of the world as depicted in the original artwork (though, again, there's no single object that matches Keats's ekphrastic account; it's seemingly a notional urn) is one of the most exciting opportunities ekphrasis gives us. In the end of my poem, looking at an image almost overwhelmed with rose petals, I ask the reader to imagine the discarded stems and thorns, and the alternate victims of that more direct but perhaps no more or less horrible violence. If Alma-Tadema's painting reflects a Victorian anxiety about being the new Rome, my poem might reflect a current American anxiety, wondering at all our pretty facades, the ugly truths hidden behind them, and the unconvincing claims to virtue made by those who do no more than bear witness.

Dan Rosenberg's latest book is *Bassinet* (Carnegie Mellon University Press, 2022). His poetry has won the Omnidawn Poetry Chapbook Contest and the American Poetry Journal Book Prize, and recent poems have appeared in *32 Poems*, *Kenyon Review*, and *Conduit*. Rosenberg teaches at Cornell University in Ithaca, NY.

ROBERT B. SHAW

Athena's Owl

I don't remember when the last time was
I sat, or to express it more precisely,
perched for an interview. My patroness
and I have been for quite a while now
out of the limelight. I suppose you'll want
to know how we crossed paths in the first place.

Well: on the brink of morning at the edge
of woods outside of what was not yet Athens,
I was taking a breather on a low limb,
about to call it a night when suddenly
she materialized, the way gods do,
right in a weed patch that my great round eyes
were scanning for some rustling thing that might
do me for breakfast, and I found myself
being fixed by *her* remarkable eyes –
the gray eyes poets always tag her with.
Gray? Turned up at me in the dawn light,
they cast a gleam like chased and polished silver
(and by the way, I'd like the word spelled "chaste").
After we had taken each other in
for what seemed like a long time, she said, "Glaux,"
(sorry, that means "little owl" in English),
"come home with me. I need someone to talk to."

Yes, I was flattered: what owl wouldn't be?
But I wasn't about to leave the forest
without some background. So she filled me in,
and I could see how seriously bleak
she had to feel, coming from such a family.
Those brothers! Sunny boy beaming mindlessly,
twiddling at his homemade instrument;
his sibling, maybe marginally smarter,
but meaner, always itching for a knife fight.

Not to mention the tomboy younger sister
out with her girl gang deerstalking all day.
Dubious uncles, too – one out at sea
brewing typhoons and hurricanes for spite;
another no one wants to think about
up to no good in the underworld.
I've sworn I'll never speak about the parents. . . .
Anyway, as night gave way to morning,
I saw she had an interesting mind
and not much outlet for it on Olympus.

So, rationally drawn as well as flattered,
I fluttered down to light upon her shoulder.
(I knew somehow, without needing to ask,
that roosting on her helmet was a no-no.)
Having agreed to be her sounding board
soon meant that I became part of her brand:
a more approachable emblem, don't you think,
than a trident or a thunderbolt? It took
a while – centuries in fact – to feel
a full-fledged member of the Pantheon.
One hard thing to adjust to was the daily
immortality menu of ambrosia,
mounds of it on gold plates, washed down with nectar.
Both food and drink were sweeter than my palate
was happy with, and left me filled but hungry,
hankering for a bite of mouse or chipmunk.
(No, I have no comment on the rumors
that I slip out for fast food now and then.)

Still, there were perks: my portrait on the coins,
and best of all, the late-night conversations
she and I had, still have, throughout the eons.
The gods don't need to sleep, so both of us
are night owls musing through the quiet hours.
What do we talk about? Whatever tempts us:
physics, and metaphysics, and these days
'pataphysics, since the state of things
keeps passing limits of absurdity.
By now we've been together for so long,
we finish up each other's sentences –
even our voices sound alike, as though

her husky one, my fluty one have met
and melded to compose a lasting chord.

We talk with resignation and sad wonder
of every fresh cohort of featherless
bipeds bent on sending Earth to its doom:
how many floods, how many epic fires
will it take to shock them into seeking
what we have to offer free of charge:
Wisdom? But there isn't much demand.
Another dispensation's oracle
that I recall in fervent fragments nails it:

Doth not Wisdom cry? . . . She crieth at the gates . . .
Hear instruction . . . and refuse it not . . .
For whoso findeth me findeth life . . . but he
that sinneth against me wrongeth his own soul:
all they that hate me love death.

                So there it is:
my own suppressed alarm put into words.
The forest I once soared in is paved over,
or else by now it surely would have burned.

Athena no doubt has her own ideas,
but when we've listened to the news each night
I can see that she's troubled. We're retired,
after all, passing time with crossword puzzles,
but each of us still misses being useful
to former devotees who need a way out.
If Wisdom's not within their narrowed grasp,
even a little common sense might help. . . .

Is that enough for now? Speaking of common
sense, it's well past time for me to preen,
and if I'm lucky maybe I can hack up
my latest nectar-permeated pellet.

    This poem began for me with a sound in the night. Some months ago, late one evening, I heard an owl hooting close to the house – something I had not heard here before, since I moved in almost four years ago. It was a mild, companionable sound, somehow like the start of a conversation. Over the next several nights I heard it again until, maybe with the moon changing its phase, it no longer enlivened the darkness. By then I had passed through a number of phases myself, in memory and reflection. I have always been fond of owls while only rarely having close contact with any. Thinking about owls and their lore made me recall something I had in a hoard of keepsakes when I was a child: a replica of one of the ancient coins of Athens, with its tutelary owl filling its obverse. From there, a chain of associations led me quickly to Athena and her . . . pet? Sidekick? Mascot? Avatar?

Classical mythology, for millennia, has offered countless poets an archetypal source, whether for flights of imagination or bouts of moralizing. I am no exception. Although I was familiar with the iconography pairing the goddess and the bird, I realized I had never come across an account of how their relationship came about. I decided to provide one, and almost simultaneously decided that Glaux would be the speaker of this dramatic monologue. That meant creating a voice, and although this probably seems a bit off the rails, I think the hooting I had heard outside my window – measured, intimate, self-assured – supplied something of the tone I wanted.

Owls often appear as humorous figures (think of the one winking on *The New Yorker*'s masthead, or the one whose eye stares intently from a bag of Wise potato chips); and of course speaking animals in literature serve comic or satirical purposes. The form the poem takes – one side of a celebrity interview – is comic from the outset. Some of the humor is cartoonish (and in spirit not very Classical), as in the take-downs of Athena's relatives. Within the comic frame, though, is the underlying import of what the goddess and her owl symbolize: wisdom, to which people pay lip service when convenient while disregarding it in the main. After the middle section of Olympian gossip, the poem becomes graver toward the end, incorporating lines from the King James Bible's Book of Proverbs. The point, I suppose, is that wisdom is not the sole property of any single culture, reverence for it and neglect of it being common to all humankind. A heavy message, adding weight to the hoots of a little owl.

Robert B. Shaw is the Emily Dickinson Professor of English Emeritus at Mount Holyoke College, where he taught for thirty-three years. He is the author of *Blank Verse: A Guide to Its History and Use* (Ohio University Press, 2007) and of eight books of poetry, the latest of which is *What Remains to Be Said: New and Selected Poems* (Pinyon Publishing, 2022).

R. ALLEN SHOAF

Rendering *Aeneid* 3.415

tantum aevi longinqua valet mutare vetustas

Easy to paraphrase, frustration itself
To translate, this line teaches us how Vergil
Endures in poetry and the culture of words.

We could almost dismiss it as filler:
"So much distant ages of time can change" –
Or, charitably, we might call it "stock."

But we'd perhaps be ahead of ourselves.
Vergil willed the poem to be destroyed, it's true,
But this line doesn't number among its faults.

Here's the line in the nude, so to speak:
"So much of time far off is able to change age" –
We may scratch our heads and wonder about it,

But we hear the challenge to his language.
Time is not the point. Change is the real crisis.
And yet we recognize change only through time

So the line insists on time and its magnitude.
The line is weighted down with the crush of time –
We can hear this when we read it aloud,

Especially in the final two words.
Some would declare that this is Vergil's style,
But I'm not writing a prosodic critique.

I desire to feel the secret of change.
Change is the bastard child of memory
Begotten upon time careless of life.

Memory fathers change on time mindless
Of the incest it indulges with chimera
Of its own fantastic metamorphoses:

The offspring of a mind obsessed with now,
A lover who mocks the sexual real,
Cries of lust forlorn, children lost, love interred –

No Troy without the stigma of "New,"
No Lavinia without Creusa's ghost,
No mother without Venus vanishing,

No father without shoulders weary of him,
No son without a hostage to fortune,
No ascent without nightmarish descent,

No empire without Dido's curse and disdain,
No ideal without human helplessness . . .
So deep the ruthless changes of remorseless time.

    Writing this poem continues an effort begun over sixty years ago when I first started reading Vergil in ninth-grade Latin and felt transfixed as well as mystified by the beauty of his language and the extraordinary passion he could convey in what oftentimes seemed to be the simplest phrases regarding the most basic of circumstances. To this day, I still don't really understand how he manages to do this – that is his greatness as a poet, I assume – but there are times when I feel I come a little bit closer to recreating the passion and the wisdom that seem to me to live in his lines.

I am of an age now to have at least a basic understanding of how hard he must have worked, how carefully he must have listened, how bravely he must have committed words and sounds to the ideas in his mind and spirit.

The current poem is one of many in which I have tried to reach and express the spirit that he lifts up in me both as a writer and as a man. Obviously, it's inadequate, but it isn't trivial.

R. Allen Shoaf is Alumni Professor Emeritus of English in the University of Florida. His most recent publication is a chapbook of poems entitled *Call Me Queequeg, Ishmael*, a response to Herman Melville's two great novels *Moby Dick* and *Billy Budd*. Recently he also published the volume, *Selected Poems 1968-2021*, a collection of several hundred poems written between his twenties and his mid-seventies. He has published scholarly papers on Lucan, Lucretius, Vergil, Ovid, and Dante over the course of his career.

GERALD SMITH

Miasma

Phrygio fallax Maeandria campo
errat et ipsa suas decipit unda vias
  – Propertius, *Elegies* 2.34

Miasma, brother to Maiandros,
When did you leave great rivers behind
Forsaking the bends and turns,
The deep current, the meanders?
Did Maiandros leave you in his wake
There on the high plains of Caria
Where he doubled the river again and again,
Bypassing old channels, cutting new ones,
Cutting off oxbows, creating islands
Until the water lost the sea?
The temple maidens saw shrines fall,
Saw Maiandros turn again before
Stones were set for the next one,
And when the swamps appeared
Was that the first time you knew peace?
In those muddy marshes
Did the swamp gas seem like breath to you
If only because it was truly local?
Were you searching for home,
Feeling those vapors wrap around you
Like a mother's worry,

Knowing in your heart, for the first time, you belonged,
That you would challenge any god or mortal
Who came to clear the air,
Cut canals, get the water moving?
And did you terrify young Hercules
Render him his first defeats,
Make him flee westward from Anatolia?
So now you hover over lowlands
Like vultures shadowing carrion –
Dark dank foul suffocating vapor,
Breath of death, sigh of darkness.
Was that old visitor
Who flew Egyptian skies your brother too
Or mentor from on high
Sent to teach you the subtleties of insinuation,
How to avoid bloody lintels,
And render death universal
Missing none of the firstborns?

"Miasma" grew out of my teaching at the University of the South. My classes involved the cultures of the Ancient Near East and East and South Asia. I sought to employ the archaeology of material remains and of ideas from these cultures in the classroom. Later my teaching involved environmental issues, and again I employed classical illustrations in these classes. I have a special interest in rivers, meanders, and swamps, and I used the imagery of both Miandros and Miasma to comment upon what we observed on field trips to rivers. The fact that my university (often called "Sewanee") was founded on a high plateau to escape noxious vapors (of yellow fever and malaria) lent some sense of local history to the imagery of miasma. The folded history of old rivers also seemed an apt image of my academic life as I closed my teaching career, which I described in this way in my last lecture: "Sewanee is a river flowing along and leaving in its curves the meanders of its history. Meanders become oxbow lakes and are cut off from the main channel. In time the oxbows become swamps or bogs and eventually fill in and disappear as active parts of the main river. The river bends again and flows elsewhere even while the meanders and oxbows remain as the braided history of sedimentation – or in the case of this analogy – remain as the textured history of old classes and old professors which have now been overlaid and supplanted by the new life of the flowing river of learning . . . The river is moving on, folding what I have done into the life, memory, and then in time, into the forgetfulness of this place." Meanders and the associated miasmas of river bottoms have supplied a rich metaphorical source for my teachings about both history and nature.

Gerald Smith is Professor Emeritus of Religion and Environmental Studies at the University of the South. He is the author/editor of a dozen volumes of institutional history, and his essays have appeared in *The Sewanee Review*. His interest in rivers derives, in part, from his passion for flyfishing. The meanders of rivers (and the noxious air of river bottoms) found convergence both in his fishing and in his teaching. Upon retirement, his writing efforts returned after many decades to his first love of poetry.

WILLIAM E. SMITH III

Ganymede

Even now, we all know the tale as *they* told it.
Hermes to Homer to Hesiod,
Until even Ovid couldn't resist my lure.
But how I changed in the telling.
So I called him daddy once. Fine,
Twice or thrice. So, he was a bit older.
But what god isn't, right? Sure, Zeus said I was young,
So young, younger than I really ever was.
But then how young, to him, I must have seemed.
When it happened, I was the age Paris was
When he wanted Helen. But Zeus had a story
To sell to humans, to gods. I wish I'd seen them,
Apollo, Eros, Poseidon, jaws slack
At the thought of the first taste.
In these tales, was I not a meal?

Now let *me* tell you about that first date.
Remember this: Even as an eagle,
He drank *my* mead, beaked mouth agog,
Wanting, waiting for it to spill over.
Eagerly he yearned for all I had to offer.
That night was no accident, no off flight
Of fancy. My father and I dreamed of kingdoms,
He his namesake city, and I?
What did I dream of? A kingdom without walls
Or limits. My father thought I was feckless.
I him foolish. I knew already time
Was not for me. So I plotted. Got my hands
On some moly, black root and milky flower,
Mixed it and drank. Made it make me more
Of myself: my beauty already thick and heavy.

With that, I gave Cronos the slip.
It was my first move. Immortality was a gift
I gave myself. Zeus only wished he had,
Though later he did grant me the stars
And Olympus. I can't fault him
For being tightfisted. But I digress.
Back to that night, that field where
I played rustic, played shepherd, played

The part I knew I needed to catch his eye.
Alone in the night, like a rare delicacy on a plate,
Ready for the taking. On that plateau,
I lounged, my tunic slipping slightly off my shoulder.
How little, how light I must have seemed
To a god. As someone would later say,
All the world's a stage.

Being a morsel that talons and a beak could snatch up –
That was my second move. Seized? As if
I didn't offer that eagle *my* mutton,
The flanks, indeed the best cut. Remember this:
He tasted what I wanted to give. Yes,
I got it both ways, but then again so did he.
Zeus found me innovative. As I invented mead,
So too did I develop delights for Olympus,
Earthy and meaty, sweet and sweaty.
I danced for him. In my final move,
What I brought to the table was often a surprise.
There's a reason I became heaven's cupbearer;
Better yet got my own constellation.
In the tales, it sounds as if one father takes from another;
But that night, it was I who took and never let go.

I did not set out to write this poem. I have been working on a playful poem series about the zodiac. After writing one for Aquarius, I was disappointed with what I had generated. So, I started over. I wondered if it would be helpful to center the poem on the figure of Ganymede given that he stands behind that sign the way Chiron is said to stand behind Sagittarius. I did not get my wish.

In a delightful act of queer refusal, this poem grew up against expectations. Instead of helping me capture an aspect of the spirit of Aquarius, Ganymede pushed me to think about what his own story could be, as well as how this myth lives through its various iterations in the literary and artistic tradition around it.

The Ganymede who presented himself to me was sassy and bold, eager to do things, to get what he wants. Yet, the Ganymede of tradition is a bit of a non-agent. In tales, paintings, and sculptures, he is often the hapless victim of Zeus's advances. In art, these pieces are frequently called "The Rape of Ganymede" (think Rubens). And over time, some authors and artists have rendered Ganymede younger and younger until, in the hands of some, he is a toddler (think Rembrandt). All of this exaggerates the power imbalance between Zeus and Ganymede.

Of course, there is cultural and artistic value in thinking through these fraught issues. Jericho Brown's hauntingly beautiful "Ganymede" illustrates this point well (*The Tradition*, 2019). But other elements of the tradition push against those portrayals. Ganymede is, for example, the mythic inventor of mead, which hints at a creative, engaged mind. He's someone, it seems, who does stuff.

The myth also leaves us with certain questions. Why does Zeus want Ganymede to live on Olympus with him? Why make him the cupbearer? If it is about lust alone, why keep him around? It's not like Zeus was known to do that with his other trysts (rapes?). What made Ganymede different?

While thinking about these things, I also thought about how relatively common and acceptable age gaps are in same-sex male relationships. My mind went to the daddy/son dynamic among some adult gay and bi men. Then there is the whole question of what is the relationship between age and maturity – and how that might look different in the eyes of various people, even those who are partnered.

Finally, what would happen then if we took Ganymede, rather than Zeus, as the protagonist in this tale?

My poem is one attempt to answer these questions.

William E. Smith III (Will) lives in Bloomington, IN, with his dog Buddy, a fitting name given by the Owen County Humane Society. Will holds a Ph.D. in Religious Studies and works in academic advising at Indiana University. He has worked on poetry off and on since he was a teenager, and returned to it with vigor during the pandemic.

C. LUKE SOUCY

Prelude to an Aubade

According to antique notions of botany
the heliotrope will soon have something to look at
        as, I am sure, would we all

if an honest-to-god chariot with an honest-to-god god
        really sprang from the sea on the horizon,

but the one I'm wondering about this morning
is the woman behind and before the man:
saffron-robed, rosy-fingered Dawn – her two claims to fame
which sound nice and all but are probably small solace
        since her son's dead and she's married to a cricket.

Yet if what I'm seeing really is her fingers
in tints at the edge of the world,
she is also enormous, and it's some trick to square
her sphere-dwarfing, sky-covering size
with her inexorable transience, her being defined
        by her always giving way.

Unlike Flora, Fortuna, and the simply Good Goddess,
she has no temples. This isn't about her.
        "O pink-digited, celestial usher," I cry,

"Pray, how shall we worship you?
You fade so slowly, where do you go?
        Seen Twilight recently?"

No reply, she is busy out vindicating roosters
and insomniacs who've made it this far. There are,
before all, better things to do than answering questions
    or prayers

like shedding light on the situation.
Is she gone yet? I can't tell.
Oh then, very well.
    Here comes the sun.

    "Prelude to an Aubade" expresses my longstanding fascination with the goddess Dawn. This arose out of a scene from Ovid's *Metamorphoses* where, in the wake of Hecuba's tragic saga, Dawn stars in a seemingly slight vignette on the death of her son Memnon. Begging Jupiter for some memorial to her fallen child, she cuts herself a pitiful figure, all but unworshipped and lacking the divine might to transform the world on her own. She is similarly helpless, in her other famous myth, to halt the eternal aging of her husband Tithonus. For a supposed deity, these are stark contrasts, combining profound powerlessness with immense emotional power.

    This tension drew me particularly given Dawn's omnipresence throughout the mythos. In Homeric ubiquity, "rosy-fingered Dawn" is up there with "wine-dark sea," yet when she shows up, it is almost always just to signal the passage of time: after all, what is dawn but the sun's harbinger? Poets writing about her from Sappho to Tennyson to A. E. Stallings naturally take Tithonus as their focal character.

    This poem, then, is my unnatural attempt to dwell with the goddess awhile, aware as I am that her point is to pass us by. For if anything is "divine" in the colloquial sense, then – beautiful, transcendental, unfathomably vast – Dawn is surely it. Bearing in mind Wordsworth's poignant plaint in "The World is Too Much with Us" that modernity has drained the world of pagan wonder, I sought to take her godly nature literally, searching for her myths in the dew of morning before losing her (sadly, inevitably, but definitionally) in the rising of the sun.

C. Luke Soucy is a translator, university bureaucrat, and vocal Minnesota native. His verse translation of Ovid's *Metamorphoses* was recently published by University of California Press; other writing, ranging from light verse to classical scholarship, has appeared in *Arion*, *Light*, and on Poets.org. Queer, biracial, and generally formal, Soucy is currently picking away at a translation of Silius Italicus's *Punica*. He graduated from Princeton University in 2019.

DAVID SOUTHWARD

Sappho at the Beach

Slick with lotion, bellies of women dozing
swell and sink. The palms of their feet find coolness
burrowing in sand. As a draft of pooled heat
nibbles the ocean,

Zoë turns to me with her burnished body.
"Let's clean up," she snuffles, "and get some dinner."

Always famished, this one. I pass her sweet grapes,
watching her seize one

nimbly in her teeth and detach it. Crushing
juice from flesh, she closes her eyes and praises
Earth for grapes and beautiful women. "Itch!" she
squeals, so I scratch it –

buttered skin, too teased where the curl of ringlets
grazes neck and back. On a whim I press her,
"How about a swim?" For I've spied another
Nereid easing

hips through sea foam, wading to deeper water.
Goddess, what unrest are you contemplating?
In she goes: head plunging, then bobbing up for
air, as a poem

breathes itself afloat. The momentum takes her
farther out than planned, where she gathers ocean
into outstretched arms – and with swoops of cupped hands
splashes her bosom.

Zoë, clucking, signals her disapproval.
Beauty's hex has waylaid me once again: drugged
reason, disarmed pride – while my heart, in pieces,
clings to the orchid

of some witch of sex for its bold labellum.
Goddess, help me! Guide me toward your secret
wisdom, sealed in coconut-scented creases
softer than vellum.

Sappho fascinates me. Not only is she the mother of lyric poetry; she is a queer icon, the adopted mother of modern lesbianism. I wanted to write a poem that captured this duality – using the meter that bears her name. I chose Swinburne's Sapphic stanza because of its bubbling, oceanic rhythm. By taking on Sappho's persona and allowing gentle enjambment to create a narrative across the stanzas, I hoped to create a compelling portrait of the amorous poet as conflicted sensualist. She feels equally drawn toward the "Nereid's" restive beauty and toward the more familiar charms of Zoë, her Toklas-like companion, who represents life in its most mundane yet lovable form. The scene hovers between ancient Lesbos and a modern resort (think Ibiza, Aruba, Cancun) to highlight the trans-historic relevance of Sapphism. While the tone may be whimsical and flirtatious, Sappho's prayer to Aphrodite is in dead earnest. I see her as a woman plagued by beauty and bewitched by eros, as most human beings are, yet trusting in the wisdom (or mercy) of the gods to see her through.

David Southward teaches in the Honors College at the University of Wisconsin-Milwaukee. His collections include *Bachelor's Buttons* (Kelsay Books 2020) and *Apocrypha*, a sonnet sequence based on the Gospels (Wipf & Stock 2018). David is a two-time winner of the Lorine Niedecker Prize, and in 2019 his poem "Mary's Visit" received the Frost Farm Prize for Metrical Poetry. He resides in Milwaukee with his husband, Geoff, and their two beagles. Read more at davidsouthward.com.

A. E. STALLINGS

Hippiad: A Verse Lecture

If Pindar sang horse races what should hinder
[Her]self from being as pliable as Pindar
                                – Byron

    ἀελλοπόδων θύγατρες ἵππων
                                – Simonides

O Pegasus, show me the first who died –
Not those who came to pillage and destroy,
Those cut down in their stubbornness and pride,
But mules foaled on the windy plain of Troy.

Dawn gallops with her gold foals up the East.
Light spreads. Diseases start, from beast to beast,
And spread to man, and spread and spread and spread
Through failures of leadership. The first to die
Were mules, mules that are half-breeds, like the heroes
Who are part mortal and part god – half mire,
Half aether, likewise mules, half thoroughbred
For pedigree, a jack-ass for a sire.

Epic has no room for donkeys, though.
They aren't heroic in their size or strength:
The peasants of the equine world, too slow,
Long-eared, ridiculous, hee-hawing, crass,
Too humble for our high-falutin' verse.
Only a simile, drawn out at length,
Has room for one: describing an attack
By Ajax, likened to a stubborn ass
Unmanageable by little boys, who whack
His back with sticks (these are the Trojans now):

The children tug and push, they cry and curse.
He munches his fill of grain in someone's field.
It's comical, how Ajax will not yield,
Stubbornly killing and killing them from the prow.

Achilles' immortal horses have been sung:
A mermaid's dowry. They will never die,
Belius and Xanthus – call them Dapple and Roan.
Even now they must be somewhere, in a field,
Flicking off mortal horse flies, nose to tail,
Beside an interstate, and diesel fumes.
They could tell us the future if we asked,
Tears running down their muzzles. We drive on
Like Achilles, pretending that the known's unknown,
No Doomsday clock now counting down to zeroes.

Stunned by grief, at the death of their charioteer
They stood just like a stele, like a stone
Set on the grave of a woman or a man,
A gravestone like a statue, of two horses
Made of marble, hard and white as bone,
Unmoveable because they had been moved,
Like limestone, down which carves a burning tear.

Pedasus was mortal, tracer horse
For the immortal horses, proud to keep
Up with their divinity. A spear
Caught him in the flank, Sarpedon's spear.
He thrashed, entangled in the reins, until
Cut loose from leather, horse-flesh, pain, and fear.

At Patroclus' funeral, four horses led
To the funeral pyre, to have their throats cut,
Falling to their knees as their throats bled,
The runnels fill with blood, darkness in glut.

Then funeral games, and at the chariot race
Nestor's son speaks harshly to his team:
"Don't let yourselves get beaten by a mare!
Run slow, and Nestor himself will slit your throats."
His words crack like a whip ripping the air.
Now they're running, now they're on a tear

Since they've just witnessed equine sacrifice,
They get it: he won't have to tell them twice.

Andromache's a horsey girl, she feeds
Her husband's team their mush of barley and wine
Before she serves her husband's meal, will muck
Out stalls, and curry coats until they shine.
She calls out: Sunbeam, Sparkle, Lightfoot, Blaze!
She loves them, but she also knows in war
They are her husband's speed to safety, prays
Her care pays off, and brings him horse-shoed luck –
If he should die, to whom would she belong?
Yet from the wall she sees – it can't be true
His body dragged behind them – or just two –
Yes, there's a roan, a dapple – splendid steeds –
Where are the others? Why a pair, not four?
But these are the wrong horses – all is wrong!
She does the math. She falls down to the floor.

At the end, two mules are hitched up – Ha and Gee,
Git Up and Whoa – they know no names but these,
No kindness but the odd slap on the rump
And a dead war horses' ration of barley. Brawn
Is what they were bred for. Engendered, they are sterile:
A mule knows nothing of a parent's sorrow,
How grief uncouples thought from mortal peril.

The way that Homer hitches up the wagon
Is so complex, there are words that only appear
In Greek here once – hapax as Gordian knot,
Singular, the plural turned to one:
Perplexity that cannot come undone.

A ransom of treasure's heavy, even so
Lighter than the dead weight that a corpse is
When the wagon bumps and bucks at every stone.
Dawn's chariot roars out of Asia's throne
Drawn by palominos, whose hooves fire
The plains and the gold ridges where the gorse is.
The dactyls rattle along, till the last whoa,
Mules dragging back the firewood for the pyre,
And the last words: Hector, breaker of horses.

This poem, or verse lecture, came out of a pandemic-lockdown obsession with the equids of the *Iliad*. I was thinking about how Western literature starts with this zoonotic plague, and then about how the first deaths in the timeline of the poem are not even of men, but of mules, and then about how "horse" is embedded in the last line of the poem; in short, how equids frame the work. Then I started reading through with an eye to individual horses and horsey similes and episodes. I was interested in how horses and other equids mirror mortals and their concerns: how they can be male or female, slave or free, mortal or immortal, noble or base. Even moments where horses seem not to be present, they are: consider the nodding horsehair crest on Hector's helmet that frightens Astyanax. (That's not in here yet, but I imagine it will be.) And then of course there is the shadow of the wooden horse, not in the poem at all, but looming in the future of doomed Troy. A prose lecture came out of this, but also this "verse lecture," which I can see adding on to, including more and more of the *Iliad*'s equine episodes, almost infinitely.

A. E. Stallings lives in Athens, Greece, and is currently serving a term as the Oxford Professor of Poetry. Her most recent verse translation is *The Battle Between the Frogs and the Mice* (Paul Dry Books), and her most recent volume of poems is a selection, *This Afterlife*, out with Farrar, Straus and Giroux.

TIMOTHY STEELE

After Her Party

Burlington, Vermont, 1960

I thought she meant her hug to show
That of her friends she liked me best.
As soon as she released me, though,
She gave the next departing guest
An even lengthier embrace.
Startled and twelve, I slipped away.
The situation's saving grace
Was her not seeing my dismay.

During her party, it had snowed.
Fresh powder creaked beneath my feet
As I wound down Deforest Road
Past tall white pines to Willard Street.
High and far in the sparkling cold
(Yet near enough for me to hail),
The Great and Little Bear patrolled
Along their circumpolar trail.

They took their fate in stoic stride.
With other stars, they shared the night.
Whether a gesture signified

Affection or was just polite
Troubled them less than it did me,
Who – feeling big, then feeling small –
Had to admit that, neutrally,
The universe can hold us all.

When my brother, my sister, and I were growing up in Vermont, our parents taught us the prominent constellations that dazzled during the long winter nights. Ursa Major and Ursa Minor especially fascinated me. Why were they way up there, in such frigid conditions, when other bears were snugly hibernating in forest dens on earth? Later, in college, I learned the answer from Ovid's *Metamorphoses*. Jupiter had raped the nymph Callisto, and when she gave birth to a son named Arcas, a jealous Juno had turned her into a bear. Arcas grew up, went hunting one day, and encountered Callisto. Since she was a bear, he didn't recognize her as his mother, and he panicked when she gazed longingly at him and growled in an attempt to communicate her love. Just as he was about to spear her, Jupiter intervened and swept the pair up to heaven, transforming Callisto into Ursa Major and Arcas into Ursa Minor. Though Juno was doubly furious that her rival and her rival's child had been so grandly elevated, she couldn't reverse her husband's act. But she persuaded the ocean deities Tethys and Oceanus never to let Callisto and Arcas bathe in their waters, which is why the Great and Little Bear are always high in view at night, circling the Pole and never dipping below the horizon.

Learning their back story enriched but didn't alter my wonder at the Great and Little Bear. From the first, I intuited their nobility – their patience, adaptiveness, and constancy. Like mythology itself (and science, for that matter), they helped make the universe interesting and companionable when I might otherwise have mistaken it for something merely vast and alienating. They hinted that it was silly to want to feel, as I had done, special. It's enough that we're all significant – carriers of consciousness and participants in the mysterious phenomenon of life. Though I couldn't have articulated these ideas on the night of my friend's party, I could go on my way, and try to get over myself and become more like the admirable creatures above me.

Timothy Steele has published four collections of verse: *Uncertainties and Rest* (1979), *Sapphics Against Anger and Other Poems* (1986), *The Color Wheel* (1994), and *Toward the Winter Solstice* (2006). He has also published two books about poetry: *Missing Measures* (1990) and *All the Fun's in How You Say a Thing* (1999). The latter is being re-issued this fall by Ohio University Press in a twenty-fifth anniversary edition.

LINDA STERN

At the Jetty

You climbed the jetty leading to the sea,
and I hung back to let you try your skill
at navigating life apart from me
though you were not so far I could not still

reach for you if you slipped and fell. I know
that wasn't fair, my child upon the shore.

You've told me many times to let you go.
To say good-bye – that's what I raised you for.

You may be right. How can we tell what's true?
Antinous whom Caesar made a god
was not more loved or beautiful than you.
Yet he, unmoored, was lost. How, much more awed

and helpless than a king, shall I not fear
a sudden fate will bear you far from here?

    Antinous, born about 110 CE, was the young male lover of the Roman emperor Hadrian. He had been a companion of Hadrian's for several years when, about the age of twenty, he drowned in the Nile River. The circumstances surrounding Antinous's death are mysterious. Some commentators suggest that the death might have been a self-sacrificial suicide during a religious rite. Hadrian had been ill, and cultic sacrifices could be done to propitiate the gods in cases of illness although Hadrian himself seems to have abhorred human sacrifice. It's also quite possible that the death was simply accidental. Whatever the cause, Hadrian, overwhelmed by grief, declared Antinous a deity and set about establishing a cult and building shrines, as well as an entire city, Antinoöpolis, in his honor. Antinous was held to be the epitome of male beauty, and numerous statues of his likeness survive to this day.

    Discussions of the historical relationship between Hadrian and Antinous often emphasize the idea of homosexuality – Hadrian and Antinous constitute one of the most iconic homosexual couples in the ancient world. However, my sonnet focuses on more general themes of human love and loss – especially on the love and loss, as well as the fear of loss, involved in the parental task of letting go. The speaker in my poem uses Antinous – a legendary archetype of a greatly loved and exceptionally beautiful young person – to assert, by comparison, that no one is more cherished and more beautiful than one's own beloved.

Linda Stern's poems have appeared in *American Arts Quarterly*, *Big City Lit*, *Kin Poetry Journal*, *Mezzo Cammin*, *Minyan* magazine, *The New Criterion*, *The Raintown Review*, and other publications. Her book, *Why We Go by Twos*, is available from Barefoot Muse Press. She co-published the poetry magazine *Endymion* and was associate editor of the online poetry journal *Umbrella*. She is a co-host of the Morningside Poetry Series in Manhattan and serves on the Board of Directors of Poetry by the Sea, an annual literary conference.

HENRY STIMPSON

Jason

Why do the gods get so worked up
about our petty problems
and move us like chess pieces
in their arrogant games?

If I were Hera, I'd luxuriate
among pomegranates and peacocks.
If I were Zeus, I'd make love
to dawn-skinned goddesses.

The gods rule us, but they are ruled
by their compulsions, as am I,
sailing past the world's edge to steal
the fleece that will proclaim my throne.

Plowing the black waters,
my stout all-seeing ship
mutters low prophecies,
and Thessaly is lost in dreams.

I've been intrigued by Ancient Greece and Rome ever since I first learned about mythology in the seventh grade. I fell in love with the *Odyssey* (in English) as a freshman at Boston University, where I later, in 1970, took a classics course with the wonderfully named eminent scholar Charles Rowan Beye. I've been in poet Alan Feldman's workshop for many years, and he gives us various themes to spark our writing. I think "Jason" was probably written in response to an assignment.

I'm slightly sheepish to admit in a journal for classics teachers that my inspiration for the poem mostly sprang from the fantastic 1963 movie, *Jason and the Argonauts* – particularly the scenes where the gods high on Olympus look down on mortals and heedlessly move them around on a Zatrikion board. The prophecy-muttering Argo with a blinking eye in front was another indelible image. Then I got to wondering what Jason was thinking out at sea in the Argo, embarking on a somewhat insane journey.

Fortunately, I hadn't seen the movie in years, so my imagination wouldn't be too restrained. On the web, I learned about Hera's pomegranates and peacocks and read summaries of the original (non-cinematic) version of this immortal tale to make sure I wasn't completely off base.

I rarely write anything I'm completely happy with on the second or tenth draft, so I kept tinkering with the poem over the years, trying to hone it to the essentials. It seems I made the right revisions and choices eventually. Though the poem is free verse, I've tried to make most of the lines loosely iambic. It's a bit more fun to have a somewhat predictable beat.

Henry Stimpson's poems have appeared in many publications, including *Poet Lore, Rolling Stone, Lighten Up Online, Atlanta Review, Delmarva Review, On the Seawall*, and *Scientific American* (forthcoming). A diehard Boston Celtics fan, he lives in Eastern Massachusetts and also writes essays and humor. He is a semi-retired public relations practitioner and a longtime volunteer ESOL tutor, currently helping a fine Moldovan man speak English better.

EILEEN R. TABIOS

The Ex-Wife Becomes Galatea

But it is unclear
what happened after you fell
from Pygmalion's pedestal –
Still, clarity is a constraint –
I refuse to say you broke –
Instead, you introduce yourself
here in Napa Valley, California
where we drink wine crafted
from grapevines surrounding us –
You raise the cabernet, swirling
the melted rubies within the glass –
You sniff, you sip, you smile –
You marvel at how "tobacco, licorice,
incense emerge from the glass,
followed by hints of white pepper
and orange peel that add intrigue . . ." –
I raise the liquid of crushed skins,
sniff, sip, smile, and reply:
"Guide my brush as I paint you
shimmering within a gown
of golden sunlight" – I smile
as I drink more wine – I utter
the fate desired by many premature
wives: "Live well the life you wish
to live as you create yourself."

"The Ex-Wife Becomes Galatea" reflects my decades-long interest in Galatea, the ivory sculpture carved by Pygmalion in Ovid's *Metamorphoses*. As described by Ovid, Pygmalion fell in love with the sculpture and begged Aphrodite for Galatea to become his wife. Aphrodite agreed and transformed Galatea into a human being. Pygmalion then married her, and she came to bear a child named Paphos, either a daughter or son. In some versions, they also have another daughter, Metharme.

I've often wondered about Galatea's true nature as the myth ascribes her identity to be what Pygmalion chose for her. In Napa Valley where I live, my husband and I built a home that we call "Galatea" for ascribing a new life for her outside of Pygmalion's desires. Because our home is devoted to art, poetry, and wine (with all three elements manifesting in the poem), naming our home Galatea was our way of suggesting that the *true* Galatea was someone who became interested in those pursuits. But those pursuits are symbolic examples; the point, the poem's narrator shares, is simply the hope for Galatea to exercise her true interests and find her true self beyond Pygmalion's determination – that the true Galatea was not the statue he'd carved then immediately brought into his home but what the woman wished to become.

Nor is Galatea necessarily who the poem posits her to be, hence the narrator's concession that Galatea be the one to "guide my brush" even as "I paint you" in order to privilege Galatea's (rights to) self-determination.

The poem's diction also reflects the hope that as Galatea creates her desired self, she metaphorically becomes delicious wine from crushed grapes. Relatedly, I refer in the poem to red wine because red wine is made from dark-skinned grapes and I'd wished to introduce the notion of "crushed skins," eliding the difference between grape and human skin, the latter being what she was under Pygmalion's control.

Lastly, in an insignificant but convenient gesture, the inserted wine tasting notes (by Antonio Galloni's *Vinous*, November 2013) describe a real Napa Valley wine, in this case the marvelous 2003 Philip Togni cabernet which, after all, would please even the gods.

Eileen R. Tabios has released over seventy collections of poetry, fiction, essays, and experimental biographies from publishers around the world. Penguin Random House SEA releases her second novel, *The Balikbayan Artist*, in Fall 2024 in Southeast Asia and in early 2025 for the rest of the world, including the U.S. In 2023 she released the poetry collection *Because I Love You, I Become War*; an autobiography, *The Inventor*; and a flash fiction collection collaboration with harry k stammer, *Getting To One*. She invented the hay(na)ku, a twenty-first century diasporic poetic form; the MDR Poetry Generator that can create poems totaling theoretical infinity; the "Flooid" poetry form that's rooted in a good deed; and the monobon poetry form based on the monostich. More information can be found at http://eileenrtabios.com.

N. S. THOMPSON

Face in the Mantle

A March frost. Portent? Sign? What will they make
Of it? The world is colder to me now
And how it closes up as whispers pass
From mouth to ear. They hiss like cackling geese,
Is Caesar sick? Something is ill, I know . . .
The outward splendour still remains, but not
My heart . . . worn out . . . A quiet old age escapes
Me. Will it be today, or will they wait?
Caesar *is* sick. Perhaps they *do* suspect
And seek assurance in a public speech?
But then my tongue is powerful, is my power.
    Words, words – my able friends – what can you say?
Whatever I intend you to, I know . . .
Poor puffed-up vanities, your high ambition
Can never save me now, only condemn;
My part was too well written and well conned.
    One last campaign? The one to conquer Parthia?
One final triumph to outface them all?
Perhaps they would forgive, but could I live
To see the hollows of the haunted years
Come creeping on me? No, I cannot face

        My ghosts and much prefer the sharp drawn steel
        Instead. So Brutus, Cassius (poor fools,
        One plods in virtue's shafts, the other crawls
        In agony as long as I draw breath),
        Will death "unlooked for" come to me today?
            O Alexander, how I envied you,
        But still I sought to emulate, not cower,
        Afraid of majesty and might. How else
        To rule an empire? What, with prattling farmers?
        Only with presence and with majesty . . .
        To something with no substance, only name,
        I gave direction and command: will it
        Be shattered at a blow? But Brutus' mind
        Is turned and now his vile ants crowd the stage
        All limply mouthing "Liberty!" But Rome
        Has crossed its Rubicon and cannot be
        Turned back, the path leads to Imperium,
        Dear nephew (how I wish that you were here!).
            Yes, such magnificence the future holds,
        But Rome will have to fight for it, I fear.
        And Caesar shivers? Yes, I feel the cold,
        Come on, my left foot, right foot, to the Curia.
            What crisp air, crowds! What mercy in the cold?

"Face in the Mantle" was an experiment to see if one could still write a dramatic monologue, but immediately became a soliloquy by virtue of its particular dramatic setting. This, of course, is the climactic moment in the life of Julius Caesar, whose assassination led ultimately to the creation of the Empire under his nephew Octavian, who proposed himself as "Augustus" (that is, "great" or "magnificent").

As a soliloquy, it could be imagined to be a speech deleted by Shakespeare from his play *The Tragedy of Julius Caesar* (1599), but as far as possible it eschews a Renaissance lexis while trying to propose a contemporary rhythmic force to the speech. In fact, it is more of a modern poem in the "confessional" mode while dealing with a classical subject. The poem attempts several character shades not seen in the play. Firstly, Caesar's health (fainting fits, nightmares, "falling sickness" i.e. epilepsy), as noted by Suetonius (*De Vita* 45) after citing his "good health": *valitudine prospera, nisi quod tempore extremo repente animo linqui atque etiam per somnum exterreri solebat. Comitiali quoque morbo bis inter res agendas correptus est*. Also his premonition that he's gone too far politically and is about to suffer the consequences. Nevertheless, his pride stimulates his courage in facing them and he consoles himself that one-man rule will come to pass under Octavian.

The title is taken from Shakespeare's play (3.2.183-85) where Antony says:
    And in this mantle muffling up his face,
    Even at the base of Pompey's statue . . .
           . . . great Caesar fell.

Perhaps there is an echo of Elijah wrapping his face in his mantle (1 Kings 19:13-16) feeling his unworthiness: "And it was so, when Elijah heard it, that he wrapped his face in his mantle, and went out, and stood in the centre of the cave" (KJ). Where the prophet is thinking of the state of Israel, Caesar is equally concerned with the state of Rome and its future, but chillingly mingled in this poem with the awareness of his death.

    Overall, the poem is grounded in the vision of Caesar that Shakespeare dramatized directly from Sir Thomas North's translation of Plutarch's *Parallel Lives* (1580) – via the French of Jacques Amyot's *Les vies des hommes illustres Grecs et Romains* (1559) – where Plutarch clearly shows Caesar's contempt for the Roman *populus* that voted him into power as consul and his overwhelming ambition to replace what was the republic under his personal rule.

N. S. Thompson lives outside of Oxford, UK, and, having been a university lecturer for many years, now works mainly as a translator of Italian fiction. He is the non-fiction editor for the literary journal *Able Muse*, and his poetry is published regularly in the magazines. His latest chapbooks are *After War* (New Walk, 2020) and *Ghost Hands* (Melos Press, 2020), and a full collection, *Line Dancing*, is out from Shoestring Press later this year.

DANIEL TOBIN

The Combatants

What lame god will fashion them on his shield
as during those great, grim mythic seasons,
the bodies stacked high as a harvest-yield?

Reaper drones. Clashing switches: missiles wield
what nemeses they will on fleshly elisions.
What lame god will fashion them on his shield

that captures, sheer rigor, the raving field
and the forged mortis of the hater's reasons?
The bodies, stacked high as a harvest-yield,

extenuate in pretense, terms, and zeal –
a taming betrayal of love's brave treasons.
What lame god will fashion them on his shield

so pixel-perfect for each witness's appeal
it beggars all history's tangle of intrusions.
Their bodies stacked high as a harvest-yield

look skyward, gazing as if through a veil
that hangs, like night, before the ardent legions.
What lame god will fashion them on his shield?
These bodies stack high as a harvest-yield.

"All poetry is political," or some such variation, I hear with considerable frequency these days and almost always declaimed with the kind of dogmatic assurance that rings, at least in the academic setting, a little too resoundingly with the smug assurance of the inquisitor rather than the rueful abeyance of the inquisitive. Are all poems always political, really? The axiomatic view of such matters, I would counter, runs the risk of effacing – too often happily – the irreducibility of poetry's aesthetic purpose. After all, even overtly political poems should be judged not on their position, regardless of whether one agrees with it, but on their aesthetic accomplishment. As the Kashmiri American poet Agha Shahid Ali observed, not all AIDS poems are good poems, not all Holocaust poems are good poems, and surely not all politically urgent poems of any dispensation are good poems. Conversely, not all poems should be read for their apparently subliminal political inflections.

Perhaps such musings are the source of my own trepidation about writing political poems, though I have written such poems, and "The Combatants" is obviously one of them. Contra any trepidation, it jumps seemingly into the fray. In fact, to write the poem I had to overcome a felt resistance to the subject matter, which is fraught and fractious and, in addition to any worsening political situation, draws from the bloodlines of an ancient toxic well. Of course, that toxic well of brutal, tribal allegiance, more than any cultural or identity affiliation, is a substantial part of what we are as a species. Homer in the *Iliad* knew this, such that we find even in these later days the perfect representation for the enduringly sad determination of warring humanity in Achilles's shield. Auden saw the relevance for his own historical moment and wrote his indelible poem that probes both retrospectively and prospectively a contemporary calamity – testimony to his global consciousness. Still, in our time, one wants to avoid becoming the artistic equivalent of an ambulance chaser or, worse, endorsing a tacit complicity with a longstanding cultural virulence.

I had no intention of writing a villanelle taking as its "triggering" subject Achilles's shield forged by the lame god, Hephaestus, until somehow, I caught the cadence of the first line. "Shield" immediately conjured the rhyme with "yield," suggesting both harvests and, more disturbingly, such yields as are invested in the wielding of armaments. The first draft came relatively quickly, though as I revised, I wanted very much to turn the poem away from what could be construed as political allegiance or animus and toward an apprehension of those deeper, ineluctable sources that appear always inevitably to cancel the better angels of our nature. Revisions inevitably followed – with my gratitude to the sensitive prodding of a trusted first reader. What "The Combatants" hopes to be, in the end, is an embodiment of Derek Mahon's ideal: "A good poem is a paradigm of good politics . . . people talking, with honest subtlety, at a profound level." That should be enough for any political poem.

Daniel Tobin's poems and translations have appeared in numerous journals and anthologies. He has published nine books of poems, most recently *The Net*, *From Nothing*, and *Blood Labors*. In 2018, Salmon Poetry published *The Stone in the Air*, his suite of versions from Paul Celan. *The New York Times* and the *Washington Independent Review of Books* named *Blood Labors* a Best Book of Poetry for 2018. *The Mansions*, a trilogy of book-length poems on the lives of Georges Lemaitre, Simone Weil, and Teilhard de Chardin (Four Way Books, 2023), has been awarded the National Indie Excellence Award in Poetry, Gold Winner of the Human Relations Indie Book Awards, and is currently longlisted for the Massachusetts Book Award.

WYATT TOWNLEY

Alexandria Redux

A house of secrets rises in mid-air
where mysteries and questions interlace:
somewhere a nook, somewhere an empty chair.

In summer when you're seeking cooler air,
or winter, warmth – or just a friendly face,
a house of secrets rises in mid-air.

You never have to knock. Come home to where
your story takes a deeper turn toward grace –
somewhere a nook, somewhere an empty chair.

A certain book awaits your downward stare.
Its pathless path leads to a placeless place;
its house of secrets houses you mid-air.

A home within a book is anywhere
you are and carries you through time and space
far from this nook, far from your comfy chair.

When countries have forgotten how to care
and cruelty's contagious, commonplace,
a house of secrets rises in mid-air:
somewhere a book, somewhere an empty chair.

    Recently I was asked to write the inaugural poem for the new Lenexa City Center Library in Kansas. Alongside the requested themes of independent thought and freedom of expression, the poem would be informed by artist Stephen Johnson's magnificent two-story stained glasswork with its array of secrets – and my own take on the value and mystery of "library" that crosses time and space.

Every new library is a reincarnation of ancient libraries, rising from ashes and rubble into our hands. We think of the Library of Alexandria, Egypt's ancient seat of knowledge housing uncountable papyrus scrolls before its tragic demise. If buildings are fragile, the impulse to inquire and ponder persists. In this age of anti-education, censorship, and book burning, the library still holds center in the quest for knowledge and freedom.

    Before putting pencil to paper, I visited the construction site several times, taking pictures and talking to the builders. The land became a hole in the ground. Messy. Noisy. Machines turned and turned, digging and pushing mud and rock in that down-up sequence of excavating first, erecting later.

    Slowly the library climbed out of the earth into the sky. The poem I wrote mimicked that process, scribbling and scrabbling in the muck, finding its way into "free" verse, and after a dozen or so drafts, insisting on becoming a villanelle. While the French villanelle is no ancient form, and while the poem is informed by the library's contemporary architecture, art, and ambiance, it too needed scaffolding to stand.

Eventually, the villanelle found its footing, and I read it at the dedication of the new library – a house of secrets rising in mid-air.

Wyatt Townley is Poet Laureate of Kansas Emerita and the author of six books, most recently *Rewriting the Body* (Stephen F. Austin State University Press). Her work has been read on NPR and published in journals ranging from *The North American Review* to *The Paris Review*, *Yoga Journal* to *Scientific American*. Commissioned poems hang in libraries, including the Space Telescope Science Institute, home of the Hubble.

JOYCE WILSON

He Was on Leave

> *It was Jupiter . . .*
> *Turned off the flow of wine that everywhere*
> *Ran in the streams . . .*
> – David Ferry, trans. *The Georgics of Virgil* (13)

Was he denying proof of origin,
who might have borne the lineage of kings,
each time he gave no other name but Jack?

Was that his shadow, out of uniform,
who turned and cut across the farmer's field?
And didn't he deserve to drive a car?

Enlisted, he had sailed off like a god,
to give and take away on foreign soil
and nourish deserts with his blood to spare.

Now he returned on leave, with time to spare,
to resurrect the golden age at home
that he remembered often while abroad,

but streams no longer flowed infused with wine
where he could quench his thirst by kneeling down
to drink with gods, in beauty and in health,

and he no longer found the warming mysteries
humming through his body when he walked,
a deity who bore a human thirst.

Did we suggest that he begin each day
possessed, and tested like a god, who vowed
to prove he was no ordinary man?

He served his country not with gods but men.
Yet when he came back home, plantation-bound,
who would praise him for his sacrifice?

During the pandemic, I was inspired to review my memories about an African American community in southeastern Pennsylvania where I grew up. The open spaces and working farms ensured a kind of beauty in the landscape that haunts me to this day. Their place in it has been an ongoing mystery.

Reading David Ferry's translation of the *Georgics* and their depiction of Greece and the Golden Age helped me approach the dynamics of this rural beauty. Virgil describes a change in nature, from a place of harmony to one of struggle, as the result of Jupiter overthrowing his father Saturn. Summoning storms, setting beast against beast, hiding fire from man, Jupiter also "Turned off the flow of wine that everywhere/Ran in the streams . . ." (xii). These details illuminated aspects of the life I remember, its wealth and deprivation.

My poem is about a neighbor I was aware of as a child who has since achieved mythical status in my memory. He had a regal bearing, physical charisma, ambition, and love of alcohol, which, without the structure of daily life in the army, sometimes got the better of him. How he would have loved partaking in the good life of ancient Greece, especially before the battle of the gods, between father and son.

I have been meeting with high school classmates, who are also interested in connecting the dots between the present and the past, and can verify that their forebears had been slaves, something we never would have asked about in school.

Joyce Wilson is editor of the internet magazine, *The Poetry Porch* (www.poetryporch.com), which has been online since 1997. Her poems have appeared in many literary journals, among them *The Hudson Review*, *Alabama Literary Review*, and *Poetry Ireland*. Her sequence of poems, "The Octagonal Schoolhouse," won the Samuel Washington Allen Honorable Mention Prize from the New England Poetry Club in 2023.

JESSICA WOOD

Odyssey 5

In sleep the green salt sea sprouts water lilies
from the foam, and squalling gulls transform
to birds whose melodies he used to know.

His bleached hair darkens and his teeth regrow.
Splintered sinews knit themselves to bone,
and scars of salt and sunburn slough away.

His years retreat with the outgoing tide;
his narrow raft becomes a skiff to home.
The constellations rise in retrograde.

The ocean licks against the green-clad sand.
The sun's hand burns against his back,
but when he lifts the water to his lips

(the water tastes of nothingness), a breeze
trades gooseflesh for his sudden sweat.
Every oxbow bank looks like the last;

the orchards in the distance raise no scent.
Where home should be, the ocean bares its face.
The foliage consumes the shadowed banks.

One moment day, the next the sun has set.
The raft beneath him fights his wish to steer,
Around him the chill wind begins to moan,

his mottled hands grow clammy in his fear.
The dawn comes without light or heat or song,
and still he marks his course and ventures on.

The *Odyssey* is a book of transformation and translation, and in this piece I particularly tried to investigate the changes that Odysseus's physical body experiences at the hands of Athena. She makes him young to meet the princess Nausicaa and ages him to deceive the suitors. Narratively, the story also shifts through time, doubling back on itself to reconsider the prior events. This recursion forces the audience to hold multiple timelines simultaneously and encourages continuous recontextualization. This poem attempts to reflect this fluidity while evoking the physical and emotional storm that Odysseus experiences before he begins, once again, to journey home.

Jessica Wood was born in South Africa, and she received her BA in Latin from Hillsdale College and her MAT in Latin & Classical Humanities from the University of Massachusetts Amherst. She is a Latin teacher at the Dana Hall School in Boston, MA. Her work has also been featured in *Just Poetry!!!*, *The Tower Light*, and *The Lyric*.

Dwelling in Possibility: A Dialogue between Editor and Artist, Student and Teacher

Philip Walsh is Chair of the Department of Classics at St. Andrew's School (Middletown, DE). He is editor of *The Classical Outlook* and previously edited *Brill's Companion to the Reception of Aristophanes* (2016).

Emma Hunter is the illustrator of *The Classical Outlook*. She graduated from St. Andrew's School in May 2025 and attends Vanderbilt University (Nashville, TN). She is a studio artist, working primarily in pen, oils, and watercolors. The following dialogue took place on April 10, 2025. It has been edited for clarity.

Philip Walsh (PW): What originally drew you to studying Latin and the ancient world as a young person?

Emma Hunter (EW): I'm thinking about this question in three parts. In middle school I took Spanish, but I wasn't the best student. I had also taken French, but my parents said that Latin would help my writing, and I enjoyed writing, and so I thought that this would be a practical way to improve my English. So that was one of the big reasons that I took it. Then the second reason was the history. In middle school before I studied Latin, I took world history, and my favorite section of that class was when we were talking about the Roman Empire. I found it so fascinating, and it made me excited to think that history was something that I would learn about while studying an ancient language. Finally, there was the mythological element of studying Latin. Growing up, I was a big reader, and I loved the Percy Jackson books. I loved the mythology and all the storytelling, and those things also inspired me to learn Latin.

PW: Yes, your response reminds me of why I started studying Latin. When I was a young boy, I found a copy of *D'Aulaire's Book of Greek Myths* in a stack of books in my house. I started flipping through it, and while I didn't necessarily understand all the myths and the references, I was fascinated with the beautiful illustrations—pictures that conveyed big ideas. After that it was the history, and at the encouragement of my parents, I started taking Latin. My origin story relates to text and image—the reception of ancient material in the modern world—so I'm glad that this collection of poems, which is interspersed with your illustrations, allows you to reflect on those original inspirations. What were your initial reactions to reading the poems, thinking about the ideas, looking at some of the visual images that are included in the collection?

EH: Yes, I was immediately impressed with the variety of poetry. When I first opened the special issue, I was expecting it to be poetry about the myths themselves, but I was interested in the way that a lot of these poets took these stories and applied them to modern day. And I was very interested in the ties between the two. And so that was something that immediately struck me. I also love reading poetry, but sometimes a poem can feel like it's floating in space, so the postludes were a great way to ground the reader in a context: for instance, why did the person create this poem? This context is helpful in understanding the poem and shaping the reader's perspective on the poem. At the same time, some of these poems reshaped my perspective on certain stories that they were retelling.

PW: Yes, reading the postludes, one realizes that an individual had a lifelong engagement with an idea—that is, they encountered a myth when they were young, and then now as an adult they are coming back to it and creating a poem that reflects on that engagement, or how their understanding has changed over time. Or one learns how a myth might relate to a poet's own life experiences: remembering a relative, a teacher, or a stranger.

EH: One of the poets [Julia Nemirovskaya] that I was drawn to does not write in English, and I didn't realize that the process of poetry and translation could involve close conversation between translator [Boris Dralyuk] and poet. Their postlude shed light on that exchange in an interesting way.

PW: And two of these poems [Balmer's "A Different Growth" and Rosenberg's "The Roses of Heliogabalus"] engage explicitly with the visual. The form of "The Roses of Heliogabalus," for instance, seems unusual and perhaps even obscure when you're first looking at it. But then you realize that the poem is actually responding to Alma-Tadema's nineteenth-century painting and that the two must be understood together. The postlude helps here as well. And that's why I also liked including your art in this collection, illustrations that you've been drawing for *The Classical Outlook* since 2023. In fact, when Rachel Hadas and I first thought about bringing this book together, we thought that your pieces would be essential. Now that you have the issue in front of you, talk about your creative process. What are your inspirations or motivations for drawing?

EH: I'm someone who is inspired by the visuals all around me or from reading a passage that's breathtaking, or even going somewhere and seeing something that's inspiring. My first thought is I want to recreate that, and this can be very daunting because it's hard to reimagine something that's already beautiful or emotionally stirring. But I want the images that I create to have hidden, mysterious qualities.

PW: I imagine that it's hard as an artist to identify your best or favorite illustration, but is there one piece about which you could say more? Many people have said to me that the spider is their favorite, in part because of the level of detail that they can see in it and the shape of the animal itself—the eye that's in the abdomen of the spider and the needle and thread. So it comes together well.

EH: Another one of my favorite illustrations was inspired by the myth of Orpheus and Eurydice (*Metamorphoses* 10.1-85). When we were reading Ovid a couple of years ago, I distinctly remember doodling in class, and then my doodling turned into something more detailed and interesting. And then I thought that this was something that I could draw for *The Classical Outlook*. I like the moment where Orpheus and Eurydice are climbing up the path and they almost reach the real world, and I kept wondering what the underworld looks like. It must be dreary, and the path must be steep and winding, but at the same time, the moment feels hopeful because the sunlight was shining into the underworld.

PW: Perhaps my favorite illustration is "Laus Temporis" ["Praise of Time"] in part because you did a lot of research on ancient temples like the Temple of Apollo at Delphi. We also read and discussed Rilke's sonnet "Archaic Torso of Apollo," and you discovered Rilke's fascination with Orpheus. All of this—your engagement with myth, history, material culture, literature, philosophy, and reception—can be read into your art.

EH: This is what I love about the classics: ideas are constantly building off each other, like layers of artwork. It starts with an original story, and then someone's writing a poem about it, and then someone creates a piece of art. And maybe in the future, my art will inspire someone who will write a new poem.

PW: Well, now I'm thinking about layers. Initially you worked on these illustrations for publication in *The Classical Outlook*. The special poetry issue of the journal was published in the fall of 2024. Then in January 2025, we celebrated the release of the poetry issue with an event at Princeton University where you and I, along with Rachel Hadas, Meredith Bergmann, Chris Childers, A. E. Stallings, and Luke Soucy, had the chance to come together to talk about poetry and the creative process. As the youngest person on the panel, what were some of your takeaways from that event?

EH: Well, I was in awe because I was surrounded by people who had an expansive knowledge of ancient literature and modern culture. There were so many references to Latin, Greek, and poetry in translation. I found those exchanges very impressive, and it made me realize how wide the classics world is. I was also thinking about what the classics carries into our world today. Each poet discussed how their craft can speak to a modern audience. As a Latin student, I'm constantly asking myself, "Why is Latin important?" And I think that that was something that we were reminded of—that is, how the lessons and feelings that are conveyed through this poetry, the lessons that are in these stories, what do they have for us today? And I think that was a takeaway from my experience at Princeton.

PW: Any final thoughts on your experience working as an illustrator for *The Classical Outlook*? Since you're about to graduate high school and go to college, will you continue to develop your artistic talent?

EH: I am always going to be wanting to create something; that's just a part of who I am. I've been drawing since before I can remember, and I think that that's going to be how the rest of my life is. I can't picture it a different way. The trial and error of the artistic process is also something that has taught me a lot of life lessons. When I'm working on a piece and I'm frustrated, I've learned to step away and come back to it at a different time. That's been my relationship with art—a constant, obsessive working on it for hours straight and then not touching it for a week. So I wish I could be more consistent because I am also a person who's always wanting to get better at the work that I'm doing. I hope to continue to take classes and to go to places that inspire me, and I hope this will make the process of back and forth feel more consistent.

PW: Yes, what I wish for you is a continued engagement with beauty and the imagination—to dwell in possibility, to borrow a phrase from Emily Dickinson. Art is about telling a story, about creating something new, about engaging in what is human. Thank you, Emma, for this conversation. I'm excited that the readers of this little book will have the chance to examine your illustrations. Rachel and I have been so happy to collaborate with you: not only as the illustrator of *The Classical Outlook*, but also as the illustrator of this *libellus*. Thank you.

EH: Awesome. Thank you.

www.ingramcontent.com/pod-product-compliance
Lightning Source LLC
Chambersburg PA
CBHW061141230426
43663CB00027B/2990